INTRODUCTION TO ISLAMIC METAPHYSICS

INTRODUCTION TO ISLAMIC METAPHYSICS

A Contemporary Sufi Treatise on the Secrets of the Divine Name

By the Moroccan Sufi Master

SHAYKH MOHAMED FAOUZI AL-KARKARI

Translated by Yousef CASEWIT, Khalid WILLIAMS

LES 7 LECTURES

Introduction to Islamic Metaphysics is published by the nonprofit organization Anwar and its publishing house **Les 7 Lectures**

44, Fernand Brunfaut Street
1080 Brussels, Belgium

ISBN: 978-2-930978-58-1
Deposit number: D/2021/14.291/08 (Belgium)
Legal Deposit: September 2021
Front cover calligraphy: Sir Mark Allen

أعوذ بالله من الشيطان الرجيم

بسم الله الرحمن الرحيم

بسم الله الرحمن الرحيم

بسم الله الرحمن الرحيم

بسم الله

بسم الله

بسم الله

الله

الله

الله

ولا حول ولا قوة إلا بالله العلي العظيم

Table of Contents

Introduction

I seek refuge in God from Satan the accursed
In the Name of God, the All-Merciful, the Ever-Merciful
In the Name of God, the All-Merciful, the Ever-Merciful
In the Name of God, the All-Merciful, the Ever-Merciful
In the Name of God
In the Name of God
In the Name of God
Allāh Allāh
Allāh
There is no power nor strength but in God,
the Sublime, the Magnificent

Through the power of the Prayer of Abraham (*al-ṣalāt al-ibrāhīmīya*) we begin this book of ours, entitled "The Kāf of Curtains over the Secrets of the Divine Hā'" (*Kāf al-astār li-mā fī hā' al-jalāla min asrār*).

Since our Order has now completed the seven Hā'-readings and we are coming to the Lām of Contraction (*lām al-qabḍ*), the disciple must have a place in the physical world to which he may return for consolation, and to help him understand, contemplate, and remember. For it is through recapitulating with intimate friends on the Path, as well as remembrance and study, that the secrets become firmly fixed in the heart, and understanding is made easy for the disciple. Every secret has branches and derivations, and each of these branches takes the disciple to a deeper understanding. And since this world is woven from the secret's root, every particle moves in accordance with the secret that flows within it. Although we speak to you of the secret in this book, we do not divulge it; for it cannot be divulged since the secret is beyond the delimitations of letters and the forms of words.

The Lord having gratuitously favored us with the renewal of the Sufi Path in our time, we have divided the reading of the Singular Name into seventy secrets, each secret comprising ten branches. The Hā' comprises ten, as do the Lām of Contraction, the Lām of Knowledge, Separation, Union, Prophethood, and Messengerhood. The ten secrets within each of the letters of the Divine Name are divided into seven that are mass-transmitted and three that are rare. I do not call the latter "rare" (*shādhdh*) in the sense that is used in the science of Hadith, but rather because they open for the disciple the door of power through which he is able to escape from the norms of sensory perception, and display saintly miracles and supernatural events.

We never depart from the meaning of the Name in anything that we say or write. After all, the Name does not leave us for the blink of an eye or with any passing thought. It was through it that we read and learned, and now through it we teach those who have saintly aspiration, sound intention, and an attitude of resignation. God says: **Read in the Name of thy Lord.**[1]

1 Q ʿAlaq 96:1.

It behooves the reader to know that books do not obviate the need for spiritual companionship, but complement it. For the secret is taken from the hearts of the gnostics, not from their books. Their books are there in order for you to understand the secrets they have disclosed to you, and to recognize what they have placed in your heart. This is why I have called this book "The Kāf of Curtains over the Secrets of the Divine Hā'." For it does not lift those curtains, but serves as a likening and an exposition of the similarity of the curtains that you traverse in your path of understanding. In this book I explain to you in a simple manner how to traverse them, so that you do not wander aimlessly in meanings and drown in mires of doubt. These explanations are exemplifications of the curtains and veils that are cast over the door of the intellect, preventing access to understanding the secrets within the Hā' of the Divine Name. I speak in this book of the first seven secrets only, and conceal the other three because they presume a realization that delimited intellects may be unable to bear.

Read this book with your heart before your intellect, and view it through the inner vision before the outer. Swim with me in the world of the letter, that you may find something to give you peace of mind and dispel your doubts.[1]

1 The present book is a translation of *Kāf al-astār limā fī hā' al-jalāla min asrār*, which was first published in 2018 by Maṭbaʿat al-Burāq li'l-ṭibāʿ wa'l-ishhār, and reprinted by Dār al-Amān, Rabat, in 2020. We are immensely grateful to Abdullah el-Kammar for his generous support of this work.

Ode to the Shade of the Thin White Cloud

A poem that encompasses the seven secrets of the Hā' of Identity

If you are truly the Qays of love,
Then behold, Laylā has offered you a glimpse

Of her splendor; she whose beauty shines
Like the full moon in the sky of reality.

No eye has ever beheld such lustrous comeliness,
That soothes peoples' souls in delight.

My heart is inflamed with passion for her,
Entangled in the fetters of desire,

The vision of her flows through my very being;
It does not leave my heart, even when my eyes sleep

She gave me a drink from the cup of love with her hand,
And now I am neither alive nor dead.

Her scent is infused with the perfume of mystical secrets,
A sweet-smelling manifestation is received by the loved ones.

In intimate union, she let down the braid of her love,
Upon which is inscribed the covenant of the Karkariyya:

Rapture, passion, desire, lovesickness,
Truthfulness, sincerity, affection, and mercy.

Then when she drew back the veil that covered her,
The Lights of Identity shined within us;

Lights that sparkle with her aging old wine,
Reddish, intoxicating, bringing with it a tremble;

She called out, "Come hither, I have divulged my ranks!
By the cup of al-Karkarī, my reality is watered!"

A pre-eternal voice that our spirits recognize,
The day of affirmation, through the covenant of love;

A hidden voice that is sweet to hear,
Successive cycles, spheres of allusions.

She seized the bow of Lordship, and divided
The nearness of sanctity into the seven of majesty.

She possesses the arc of instruction, and we
The arc of receptivity by the Light of inner vision.

She took up the thimble of measuring, and played
The finest doctrine upon the strings of the law.

The melody of existence began to flow, and sent
The impassioned spirits into drunken rapture.

A holy melody, love itself,
Which reveals the treasures of the Hā' of Identity.

Upon the string of union, she played for us
A tune that showed us the method of our Order.

When our hearts became stirred with the music,
The inward eye awoke in us.

We saw the Light of love emanating
Upon existence, through the vessels of creation.

She flung down her staff, the soul, and knew
For certain beyond doubt that God is One.

All existence is sure to fade,
Save for the Lord, who forever remains.

Nothing is in existence except for our God,
Who is veiled by the intensity of His manifestation.

To the tune of passion, for us she sang
Of Man, the locus of vicegerency.

The spirits are the fragrance of his beauty,
For which the eternal birds sing.

It is the dot of the secret, with which is written
The pre-eternal verses of the hidden book.

Rule is his, by virtue of the secret's essence
Which the angels glorify in their supreme prostration.

A bottomless ocean, a secret concealed,
A cup that pours a draught of pure love.

The lamp of the innermost core of hearts,
The star of guidance to which spirits ascend.

His form is a meaning that bears witness
To what is hidden from us with human traits.

He is the Inhabited House of the heavens above;
Upon whose secret the Intimate Friend [Abraham]
leaned in intimacy.

In the world of bodies, he is the Kaʿba
To which all hearts make pilgrimage and obeisance.

His Light is from God's Light, flowing to creation;
For us he is the disclosure-site of supreme mercy.

He is the one, the unique, who encompasses
Everything in existence, mankind's intercessor.

He who sees him is fortunate and blessed,
And he who sees one who sees him has cause to rejoice.

When she sang of the secret of gnosis,
Our spirits were roused to the Lām of Sainthood.

We donned the holy garb of the Beloved in the presence
Of passionate love, and the sun of providential care appeared.

Immanence became for us a transcendent secret,
And humanity became the essence of Identity.

Existence became an outer inscription upon our being,
And we became its mysterious inner engraving.

We verified the reality of the soul by its secret,
Like Light flashing forth from the fire of expression.

We are the spark of the effusion of beauty,
From which all the levels of existence unfolded.

We became the center of truth-verification, by which
The unity of multiplicity is grasped.

We hearkened to the last chords of purity's tune,
Until at last it faded into darkness.

All that echoes now is the holy verse,
Has there come upon man a span of time?

No melody is sung, no tune is played,
Not even a whisper or a whistling breeze.

A cloud, no air above it, nor anything below,
Nothing there but sheer bewilderment.

Effacement and obliteration, no trace to be seen;
The door to the sciences of exclusive singularity.

That is the Sūrat al-Ikhlāṣ, wherein
Say: He is God is the most powerful expression.

One knows not who says it, nor to whom it is said;
Say; that is the separation of reality.

Then when the springs of our spirits became pure,
We saw the reality of the union of sainthood.

I ask the Lord's forgiveness for every conjecture,
Every doubt that ever formed within us.

For the strings only stirred by divine decree,
The reality of the measuring of His will.

What they played was the tune of their annihilation,
That we might grasp the meaning of with-ness.

He who contacts this reality finds salvation,
Which none would refuse but one devoid of reality.

The Best of Creation drew the path of union,
Plain and straight with the dear Alif of mercy.

His is the gathering of the allness of one and all,
And the singularity of the singular, the scepter of sainthood.

The Alif of the name of majesty has no corners,
In which to hide a Hell or stow a Paradise.

The substance of the strings is the prime matter of their existence,
Which the people of eternity have mercifully attained.

The secret of the basmala of existence, through which
The laws were founded and set up straight and tall.

All draw water from the dot of sainthood,
The effusion of knowledge; a Path clear and pure,

Just as the Confidant drew from al-Khiḍr,
Who showed him the pronouns of the secret of sainthood.

The science of eternity, hidden and unexposed,
Except to the Messenger or the station of prophethood.

Those are the levels of Identity in dispersion,
Which may seem to you to be few.

Seven levels disclosed to you, which leaves
Another three that are yet hidden and rare.

That is ten in all, with the perfection of totality,
Seven in the pilgrimage, three upon the return.

I gathered them in seventy verses, like the veils
That stand between the Lord and His creation.

I end them with abundant blessings and peace
Upon the best of creation, the master of mankind,

Muḥammad the city of knowledge, our beloved,
And his family, the gates to the knowledge of reality.

I – The Innermost Secret (*al-sirr*)

Wheresoever you turn, there is the Face of God.

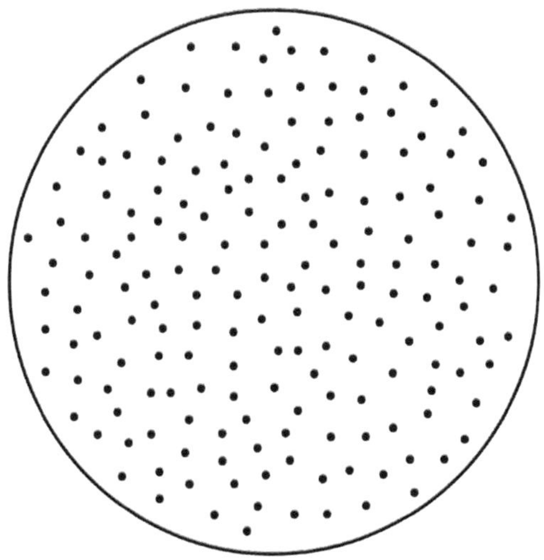

The Innermost Secret (*al-Sirr*)

The meaning of the innermost secret (*al-sirr*) in the terminology of the Karkariyya order:

The innermost secret is the subtle reality of divine mercy (*laṭīfat al-raḥma al-ilāhiyya*). This virginal reality is hallowed beyond any aspirations of servanthood which may seek to deflower it. It is stored within the kernel of the seed of the heart. The fruit that it yields is the eye-witnessing of the life-breaths of God's exclusive singularity (*aḥadiyya*), which flow through the manifestation-site of the primal self-identification of the Essence.

This subtle reality is the Divinity (*lāhūt*) that flows through all things. It appears in an imaginal form in proportion to the life that is stored within that thing; for it is the joining together of the name and the Named, and the route for the ascension of the lower self (*nafs*) to the Spirit (*rūḥ*).

This virginal subtle reality is free from contact with any aspirations of fantasy and imagination. It is the oil of mystical knowledge, distilled from the husk of all things other-than-God. These realities are subtle beyond expression, and cannot be delimited verbally or orthographically. It is a matter of sheer fruitional experience, tasted only by those who plunge the depths of the kernel of the heart.

As for the kernel (*lubb*), it is the preserved tablet of knowledge. Therein lies the root of the intellect illumined by the holy Light, where the physical eye meets the eye of the heart.

Only those who possess strong resolve may directly experience the innermost secret. They entirely orient themselves in pursuit of pure meaning, and ride upon the steed of willpower, with both a strong spiritual essence and the power of passionate love. They drink from the wellspring of life whose waters flow down from the mountain peaks of the pretemporal covenant of, **Yes indeed, Thou art our Lord**, where the breezes of the All-Merciful Cloud-Breath gently blow. Whoever is in such a state, and is accepted in pre-eternity, will witness the life-breath of the spirit of the divine command with his own eye. This spirit precludes all plurality and stands forever alone, in a state of total nondetermination and nondelimitation that is independent even of nondelimitation itself, for the Essence stands apart from the fetters of nonexistence and immutability.

Know, moreover, that the innermost secret is not something that can be spoken of, but a realization of the presence of the Real. It is the descent of the Real to the servant, and the ascent of the servant to the Real. It is a state, and a direct experience through unveiling. It is a certainty that is curtained by the "*As if*" (the Kāf) of "*As if* you see Him (*ka-annaka tarāh*)."

Attaining the innermost secret means drawing a hand's span closer to the Presence, so that the Presence draws an arm's length closer to you.[1] It is not a matter of reading the books of the Sufis and imagining that you have discovered the secret, or listening to your lower self's ramblings and supposing that something has been unveiled to you. Rather, unveiling occurs by truly recognizing your own soul, and recognizing all things through your own self-recognition. God says: **The gaze did not swerve; nor did it transgress.**[2] That is, the Beloved's ﷺ **gaze** did not **swerve** from his innermost secret at the Station of Two Bows' Length, nor did it **transgress** the boundaries of his true nature. He ﷺ recognized none other than his true nature, and saw none other than his own essence.

Now, in order to learn the innermost secret and stand at the station of its people, you must first and foremost find its wellspring. By this I mean a Shaykh who will teach you how to reach God (*al-Shaykh al-mūṣil*), and whose very sight inspires in you an understanding of the seriousness and severity of this affair. As for the seeker who cannot find the waters of realization, he

1 This is a reference to the Holy Saying (*ḥadīth qudsī*), or extra-Qur'ānic pronouncement in the divine voice: "When the servant draws a hand's span nearer to Me, I draw an arm's length nearer to Him. When he draws an arm's length nearer to Me, I draw a fathom nearer to him. When he comes walking to Me, I go running to him." Bukhārī, *Ṣaḥīḥ*, Kitāb al-Tawḥīd, #7098.

2 Q Najm 53:17 "The Prophet's **gaze** did not swerve from the wonders being revealed to him (Aj). More generally, it implies that he did not swerve away from the truth that he sought (Ṭū). Other say [the lote tree of the boundary, a tree in the seventh Heaven to the right of the Divine Throne which the Prophet witnessed on his nocturnal ascent (*mi'rāj*)] was covered with angels and butterflies of gold, which were circumambulating it (Aj, IK, Q, Ṭū)." *The Study Quran*, 1292.

is to perform the dry ablution (*tayammum*) with dust, in the manner of those who are too sick to use water. He must adhere to the outward levels of the revealed Law as understood by the average believers, and profess God's perfect transcendence, while surrendering to God's folk.

You must also know that the innermost secret is a station, not a discourse. It is knowledge that lies beyond the spirit; far be it for the lower soul to sense it, or for the delimited intellect to witness it. It is beheld by neither angels nor devils. It is knowledge that is hidden and stored away. **None touch it save those made pure.**[1] God's Messenger ﷺ said, "Verily, there is a type of knowledge that is hidden, known only to the knowers of God."[2] Verbal expression does not encompass it and therefore cannot disclose its mystery. It pertains neither to the sensory domain nor to the domain of pure meaning, yet it is at once the sensory domain and the domain of pure meaning. So understand!

To directly experience the innermost secret, you must learn to live it: you must clothe your states in it, sleep with it, and wake up to it. You must smell, taste, and feel it. You must pray and fast with it. You must observe all the prescriptions mandated by the Law while being present with it through direct experience and witnessing, until it yields to you the fruit of your incapacity (*'ajz*). This incapacity will then take you to a higher level of understanding of the innermost secret, until you arrive at the farthest limit of your spiritual aspiration. At that point,

1 Q Wāqiʿa 56:79.

2 Suyūṭī, *La'ālī*, K. al-ʿilm, vol. 1, p. 22.

the secret of the innermost secret (*sirr al-sirr*) begins.

Now, the innermost secret occurs in the disclosure-site of the letters (*majlā al-ḥurūf*) in the guise of two letters: one that is visible above the line, and another that is hidden beneath the line. Thus, for the possessor of the innermost secret, the letter of his body is fixed in the outer realm of the revealed Law, while the letter of his spirit floats through the multiple worlds of reality. He embodies the revealed Law in himself, and attains realization of what is outside himself.

The innermost secret, then, is to witness existence in a state of non-duality. It is to be neither near nor far. It is to be incapable of invoking Him, and to recognize Him without a trace. It is to not know Him, and to not be ignorant of Him. It is to not speak about Him, and to not be silent about Him. It is to be neither dead nor alive. It is to bring together the two opposites, to drink the two oceans, and to be the meeting place between them. It is to recognize who you are, and who He is, and who I am, and who we are. The innermost secret is to negate all things, then affirm them. It is to see that all things hallow Him through the voice of, **Nothing is as His like.**[1]

1 Q Shūrā 42:11.

He Took a Handful of His Light

Know, may God grant you success, that the majestic and sublime *Dhāt*, the Essence of the Real, precedes all relations and disclosures. It is above all verbal expressions and hallowed beyond all allusions. There is no way to say anything about It in any respect, for It stands above the letters Dhāl-Alif-Tā' of *Dhāt*, and is not associated with any ontological relationship. One can only be silent about it, because the vital breath of the letter cannot violate its sacred precinct. It cannot be qualified by an attribute, nor characterized by a description.

Know, moreover, that God's glorified Essence cannot be separated into parts, nor divided into portions, nor qualified by modalities; and whoever believes any such thing is in grave danger. Thus when we speak of the "Handful of God's Light", the word "of" denotes honor (*tashrīf*), not divisibility (*tajzī'*).

What does it mean that He "took" (*qabaḍa*) this Handful?

Anyone who has the least familiarity with this intellectual discipline knows that the meaning of the verb "to take a handful" (*qabaḍa*) denotes the first manifestation of the secret of opposites (*sirr al-ḍiddayn*). For the Essence's nondelimitation only became nondelimited when delimitation (*taqyīd*) became manifest. Thus, nondelimitation became evident through delimitation, and Light became manifest from darkness, and the Lord became distinct from the servant, and the Creator from creation. However, this opposition is not one of incompatible difference. Rather it is an opposition of compatibility, love, and servanthood.

Some may find this discourse surprising and ask: how could the Lord have become distinct from the servant, and the Creator from creation? I say: one of the attributes of the Real is the attribute of non-dependence (*ṣamadiyya*). If the servant were not servant, then the Lord would not be lord, since there can only be lordship when there is servanthood. By "would not be" I do not mean that His lordship would be nonexistent—far be it! His attributes are without beginning. Rather, "would not be" means that the lordship would not become manifest until the servant became manifest.

Now this mystery is apprehended only by those who possess knowledge of the Opening Chapter of the Qur'ān (*umm al-kitāb*, lit. the Mother of the Book); that is, those who attain realization of the Holy Saying: "I have divided the prayer between Me and My servant into two halves, and My servant shall have what he has asked for."[1] It is they, may God be pleased with them, who are given before they ask.

1 In this passage, the Shaykh is quoting the Holy Saying that is reported by Muslim and other hadith transmitters in which God says: "I have divided the prayer between Myself and My servant into two halves, and My servant shall have what he has asked for. When the servant says: **All praise belongs to God, the Lord of the worlds**, God says: 'My servant has praised Me.' And when he says: **The Compassionate, the Merciful**, God says: 'My

Similarly, the name the Creator existed in pre-eternity, but it only became manifest and evident by the manifestation of creation; and in this manner we came to know that creation was created by the glorious Creator.

Now if you know that the Handful of Light is the secret of how the opposites came to be, then you should know also that it is the liminal boundary between the two oceans, and the "Two Bows' Length." God says: **Then he drew nigh and came close, till he was within two bows' length or nearer.**[1] The Handful of Light is thus the gate of entry into the worlds of eternity, and the focal point of the gift-apportioning from the unseen world upon the notables of the world of disquietude.

Abū Hurayra narrates that the Prophet ﷺ said, "Do not name yourselves with both my name [Muḥammad] and my nickname [Abū al-Qāsim], for I am Abū al-Qāsim (lit. "the distributor"). God gives, and I apportion."[2]

The reality of the Handful is the concealed mystery (*ṭilsam*) of a solitary Alif (*alif fardānī*) which, through the secret of the Ḥā' of everlasting Life (*ḥayāt*), brings together the levels of the

servant has extolled Me.' And when he says: **Master of the Day of Judgment,** God says: 'My servant has glorified Me' and when he says: **Thee we worship and from Thee we seek help**, He says: 'This is between Me and My servant, and My servant shall have what he has asked for.' And when he says: **Guide us upon the straight path, the path of those whom Thou hast blessed, not of those who incur wrath, nor of those who are astray,** He says: 'This is for My servant, and My servant shall have what he has asked for.'" Muslim, *Ṣaḥīḥ*, Kitāb al-Ṣalāt, #395.

1 Q Najm 53:8-9.

2 Aḥmad, *Musnad*, Abī Sa'īd al-Khudrī, #9385.

vital breath of the Mīm of Muḥammad, which is as eternal as the eternity of the Dāl of the Primordial Cloud (*al-dāl al-ʿamāʾī*) that brings together the two bows (*qawsayn*) of post-eternity and pre-eternity through the length (*qāb*) of the servant who pertains to the Real (*al-ʿabd al-ḥaqqī*).[1]

What is the secret of the manifestation of the Handful?

Know, dear seeker of truth, that the Handful of Light was a hidden treasure, and the entities were absorbed in its inmost hidden center. They were nonmanifest within it just as waves are nonmanifest within the ocean. But when the tidal ebb of passionate love (*ʿishq*) within the unseen realm poured forth by the treasure's "loving to be known," then what was concealed became manifest, and what was unseen disclosed itself. Thus the Handful became evident by the sovereignty of love, and those hidden entities and possibilities cried out in yearning in the midst of their nonmanifestation: **a Messenger has indeed come unto you from among your own**,[2] and each recognized itself through the Handful's own self-recognition.[3]

Love was therefore the fountainhead of the first descent of the all-inclusive effacement (*al-ṭams al-aʿamm*) from the oceans of God's exclusive singularity (*aḥadiyya*), and from what lay

1 This spells "Aḥmad" (Alif Ḥāʾ Mīm Dāl).

2 Q Tawba 9:128.

3 The Shaykh in this paragraph is evoking the symbolism of the Holy Saying known as the hadith of the hidden treasure. It reads: "I was a hidden treasure, and I loved to be known, so I created creation, so that I may be known." ʿAjlūnī, *Kashf al-Khafāʾ*, #2016.

beyond the veils of divine exaltedness. Thus, love was the root of existence, which is why love has primacy while all else is secondary. It is also why love is superior to gnosis. Thus God says on the tongue of His blessed Messenger ﷺ: **Say, 'If you love God, follow me, God will love you and forgive you your sins. And God is Forgiving, Merciful.'**[1]

How then did those hidden entities and possibilities become distinct from each other, if their root was the one Handful?

When the Handful inclined away from the center of divine will, through the secret of yearning, it drew the line of monotheism. This was the line that was drawn in the sand by the Beloved ﷺ when he said, "This is God's Path."[2] Ponder this statement, and you will grasp the subtle allusion. Who actually drew the line? And what did he actually draw?

The Alif flows through all the letters, just as the one flows through all the numbers, and just as spirits flow through bodies. Consider the numerical sequences and you will find that they are none other than the number one which manifests in the numbers two and three. That is, two is none other than one and one, and three is none other than one and one and one. There is nothing there except for the one, which is concealed in name but disclosed in essence throughout all the numbers. Similarly, the Alif inclines, bends itself, and becomes manifest in the let-

1 Q Āl 'Imrān 3:31.

2 Tabrīzī, *Mishkāt al-maṣābīḥ*, K. al-Īmān, #166.

ters. It manifests more intensely in some letters than in others. For example, in the Bāʾ of the basmala, **It seems the same;**[1] yet in other letters the Alif conceals itself and can hardly make its meaning clear,[2] even though it flows through both the latter and the former, as God says: **till when he comes upon it, he does not find it to be anything, but finds God there. He will then pay him his reckoning in full.**[3]

1 The Shaykh is alluding to the verse in which Solomon asks the Queen of Sheba, **Is your throne like this? She said, 'It seems the same'** (*ka'annahu huwa*). Q Naml 27:42.

2 This is a reference to Q Zukhruf 43:51-52 **And Pharaoh called out among his people, saying, 'O my people! Is not the sovereignty of Egypt mine, and do these streams no flow beneath me? Do you not, then, see? Am I not better than this one who is vile and can hardly make his meaning clear?**

3 Q Nūr 24:39. The Shaykh is referring to the verse: **As for those who disbelieve, their deeds are like a mirage upon a desert plain which a thirsty man supposes is water, till when he comes upon it, he does not find it to be anything, but finds God there. He will then pay him his reckoning in full, and God is swift in reckoning.** "The **mirage** discussed here is based on the physical phenomenon cause by the difference in temperature between the warm air immediately above the hot desert floor and the cooler air above it. The warm air close to the ground refracts the light from distant objects slightly upward, giving the appearance of water reflecting the sky or other objects. Since the apparent 'water' is actually the inverted light of distant objects or the sky, one can never actually reach it; the inversion effect will gradually disappear, the closer one gets to it. **Their deeds are like a mirage** is thought to refer to the good actions of disbelievers such as acts of filial piety, maintaining good family relations, and acting well toward one's neighbor; that is, they believe there is some reward or benefit from their deeds, but ultimately there is not, because they exclude God. **Find God there** is understood to mean 'find the Recompense of God' or 'finds the Judgment of God' or 'finds the path to Him.' It also means that their deeds are not ultimately good even in this world and that what they believe to be good leads to greater corruption and error." (*The Study Quran*, p. 881).

All that is Upon it is Passing Away

Outward existence imprints its marks upon the canvas of being. Whoever looks at outward existence with his physical eye will see it as an engendered being insofar as he affirms his own attribute of being. He will observe the individual **ships towering aloft upon the** visual appearance of the **ocean** of existence and subsistence.[1] But engendered existence never was and will never be. As Junayd, may God be pleased with him, said, "That which is situated between the two edges of annihilation is itself annihilated." Engendered existence therefore only became manifest by the ripples of waves of the ocean of Real Existence. That is, engendered existence at its root is the manifestation-site where the stillness of the ocean of the Real becomes motion. For the ocean of the divine Essence is absolute stillness; it has no movement nor sound. But the waves of love caused movement in the midst of this fathomless and all-consuming stillness, and the ocean began to ripple with the motion of yearning that yielded the waves of existence.

This is all to say that anything that is qualified by location is also permeated by the property of annihilation in respect of its form, and hence it assumes the property of existence only

1 Q Raḥmān 55:26.

within an illusory world. For upon close examination, the herebelow is a dream. A tradition states, "People are asleep, and when they die, they awaken."[1] Moreover, the hereafter is a result of the herebelow, and it too is therefore a dream since its root is a dream. However, the hereafter assumes the attribute of actuality (*wāqiʿiyya*) to a greater extent than the herebelow. This is because of the descent of the realities to the outer realm of named things.

How then can illusion (*wahm*) assume the quality of actuality? And what does "illusion" mean?

In the terminology of our Order, illusion (*wahm*) denotes the power of conceptualizing forms that appear to bear a resemblance to divine incomparability, and the faculty of discernment, judgment, and the secret of Lawgiving. This is to say that illusion exercises authority over the realm of possibility insofar as it possesses authority by the whip of heedlessness (*ghafla*) upon the intellect.

Now when I say that the intellect (*ʿaql*) pertains to the levels of heedlessness, I mean the bestial intellect (*al-ʿaql al-bahīmī*) which is dominated by the appetites of the stomach, the loins, and what is subordinate to them. For whatever the intellect conceptualizes in the sensory domain is the result of illusion. This conception is similar to what occurs when a drunkard or a madman sees things that are nonexistent. Likewise, the bestial

1 Suyūṭī attributes this saying to ʿAlī b. Abī Ṭālib. See *Durar*, Ḥarf al-Nūn, #427.

intellect sees none other than the illusory conceptions of its appetites and obsessive attachments.

Know, moreover, that an illusion is the result of an outpouring from the names of the Real. It is through this outpouring that concrete entities (*aʿyān*) in existence disclose themselves. Each concrete entity in existence is sustained by one of the divine names, and discloses itself within one of the manifestation-sites of the realities of that name. Thus, the concrete entities are passing away with respect to their outward form, and subsisting with respect to their inward essence.

For instance, the name the Provider (*al-Razzāq*) has many disclosures which are evident in scores of concrete entities. The name the Provider manifests itself in food, wealth, children, and health. However, all of these self-disclosures are passing away with respect to their forms. Money decreases when it is spent, health is displaced by illness, and food spoils with the passage of time. Yet, the reality of the name the Provider subsists. It does not pass away, because it is the one of the manifestation-sites of universal reality that is referred to as the ever-remaining Face of God.[1]

Thus, the attribute of actuality (*wāqiʿiyya*) is draped over the illusory domain in respect of the glass through which it is observed, not in respect of its quiddity (*māhiya*). Whoever sees through the glass of heedlessness will of course behold concrete

1 This is a reference to **All that is upon it is passing away. And there remains forever the Face of thy Lord, Possessed of Majesty and Bounty.** (Q Raḥmān 55:26-27).

entities and existent things as clothed in the robes of subsistence, seated on the pedestal of permanence.

However, whoever sees through the glass of gnosis (*maʿrifa*) with the eye of inclusive oneness will apprehend the verse: **All that is upon it is passing away.** He will know that the pronoun "it" (the "*hā*" in *kullu man ʿalayhā fānin*) refers to anything that is qualified or confined by space. There is no exception to this, including the tiniest mustard seed or anything smaller of which God knows. Hence, **all** things are **passing away** with respect to their form. The form does not smell the whiff of existence, let alone partake in it. It is but a ripple upon the ocean of Real Existence.

Finally, the one who sees through the glass of God's exclusive singularity beholds the perishing of all things, as God says: **All things perish, save His Face.**[1] To this effect, al-Iskandarī says in one of his aphorisms: "Engendered phenomena are immutable by God's immutability, and obliterated by the exclusive singularity of His Essence."[2]

Thus, God's inclusive oneness (*wāḥidiyya*) extinguishes the attributes, whereas His exclusive singularity (*aḥadiyya*) demolishes the essences of existent things. Or as it has been said, "exclusive singularity is an ocean without waves, while inclusive oneness is an ocean with waves," even though we consider the reality of exclusive singularity to be higher than that of inclusive oneness, for it is unqualified existence that eliminates

1 Q Qaṣaṣ 28:88.

2 Aphorism #141, Chapter 14. See Danner p. 82.

all relations, considerations, determinations, and correlations. It is the unseen of the unseen (*ghayb al-ghayb*); "proximity without the Two-Bows' Length;"[1] the sheer Essence; and true knowledge with no subject or object.

1 *Qāba wa-lā qawsayn*, "He drew near two bows' length"

Wheresoever you turn, there is the Face of God

God says: **To God belong the East and the West. Wheresoever you turn, there is the Face of God. God is All-Encompassing, Knowing.**[1]

God's all-embracing vastness (*wusʿ*) is not a matter of spatial distance—far be it! God is beyond space and time, yet space and time are not devoid of Him. He is free from things, but things are not free from Him. He is neither conjoined with concrete entities, nor disjoined from them. For this reason, the reality of turning toward His Presence is not a directional or spatial orientation. Rather, it is to orient oneself through upright comportment and the affirmation of divine unity. For He is everywhere, and He is nowhere. To this effect, a poet once wrote:

I saw my Lord with my heart's eye.
"Who are you?" I ask; "You", His reply.

For in you, where-ness is nowhere;
Where you are, there is no "where."

1 Q Baqara 2:115.

You are he who occupies all "where"s;
Where there is no "where," you are there.

In my extinction, my extinction itself is extinct;
You are found where I am extinct.[1]

Therefore wheresoever you turn, that is your qibla. Do you not see that the moon can be observed from any direction you turn? Thus, the beloved Prophet ﷺ said:

"Verily, you will see your Lord as you see this moon, and you will have no trouble in seeing Him. So if you can avoid missing a prayer before sunrise [the *fajr* prayer] and a prayer before sunset [the *'aṣr* prayer], then do so."[2]

He ﷺ linked prayer to the vision of God, for prayer is a Light, and God is the **Light of the heavens and the earth**,[3] and the moon is a manifestation-site of the name the Illuminating (*al-Munīr*). He who beholds the luminous splendors of the prayer—for prayer (*ṣalāt*) is his link (*ṣila*) with his Lord—till all separative entities (*aghyār*) are obliterated, and all traces and marks of otherness are leveled away, and only the Light of the All-Forgiving Lord remains, then his prayer is an imminent anticipation of the beatific vision in the next world.

In order to clarify this meaning further, you should know that the Light of God brings together that which is imminent

1 Verses ascribed to al-Ḥallāj.
2 Bukhārī, *Ṣaḥīḥ*, K. Mawāqīt al-Ṣalāt, #6906.
3 Q Nūr 24:35.

and that which is yet to come. Whoever holds that the Light of God cannot be seen in the herebelow thereby imposes temporal boundaries upon God by appointing Him a time when He will be seen, on the Day of Increase (*yawm al-mazīd*).[1]

To this effect, one of the aphorisms of al-Iskandarī states: "Far be it for our Lord to recompense with credit the servant who deals with Him in cash!"[2] The word "credit" here symbolizes the delayed reward of the hereafter. For God is the Generous (*al-Karīm*), and far be it for Him to see you perform an act of worship now, and delay your reward until later, although there certainly will be a reward on the Last Day, as God promises in His holy book. Thus you recognize the value of the Light of God, and that He rewards His servants immediately, but their inward visions are heedless, and their hearts distracted. If only their hearts became illuminated, the concept of time itself would vanish for them, and the imminent would be the same as that which is yet to come. They would see the recompense for their deeds as soon as they performed them, for His recompense is immediate. I could go further and say that if the servant became completely annihilated (*fanā' kullī*) and divested himself of all contaminations, he would eat and drink from the Garden even while still in the herebelow.

1 The Day of Increase (*Yawm al-mazīd*) is the ultimate goal of the spiritual Path. The term is drawn from the Qur'ānic verse: **Enter it in peace. This is the day of abiding." Therein they shall have whatsoever they will; and with Us there is more/increase (*ladaynā mazīd*)"** (Q Qāf 50:34-34).

2 Aphorism #89, Chapter 10, *The Book of Wisdom*, trans. Victor Danner.

Can God be seen in the herebelow?

If the direct vision of God in the herebelow were theologically untenable, then God's Confidant, Moses—peace be upon him—would not have asked to see God, for the prophets know the sacred Law better than anyone. Yet when the Confidant asked for a vision of God, God did not prohibit him from asking. God says:

And when Moses came to Our appointed meeting and his Lord spoke unto him, he said, "My Lord, show me, that I might look upon Thee." He said, "Thou shalt not see Me; but look upon the mountain: if it remains firm in its place, then thou wilt see Me." And when his Lord manifested Himself to the mountain, He made it crumble to dust, and Moses fell down in a swoon. And when he recovered, he said, "Glory be to Thee! I turn unto Thee in repentance, and I am the first of the believers."[1]

Know, moreover, that at the moment of the beatific vision, you are neither in this world nor in the next. In fact, you have no existence in the first place, because you do not see Him with anything other than His own vision. Glory be unto Him! **Nothing is as His like.**[2] Such is the spirit of sanctity which is expressed in the Holy Saying, "I become the vision with which he sees."

So what does **Thou shalt not see Me** mean? It means that **thou shalt not see Me** except through the eye of annihilation,

1 Q Aʿrāf 7:143.

2 Q Shūrā 42:11.

because the exaltedness of divinity (*ulūhiyya*) excludes duality. Now, even though Moses' question was addressed to lordship (*rubūbiyya*), for he said **My Lord** [not "my God" or *ilāhī*], **show me, that I might look upon Thee,** Moses nonetheless aspired to have direct knowledge of divinity. But whereas lordship assures your subsistence and accepts duality, divinity annihilates you so that nothing remains but His Name. God's exclusive singularity (*aḥadiyya*) reduces you to nought, obliterates you, and effaces you, so that nothing remains but the Named. This is why **Moses fell down in a swoon.** That is, he passed away from himself and witnessed God's transcendent mystery. And **when he recovered, he said, "Glory be to Thee!"**; that is, he proclaimed God to be hallowed beyond all that is not proper to His Presence.

If you are truly someone who seeks to experience God, then the circle of certitude must inevitably move within you. For no matter how close the lover is to his beloved, he still seeks to be even closer. You must inevitably seek certitude, and certitude demands direct witnessing. That is why Moses the Confidant of God said, **My Lord, show me, that I might look upon Thee,** and why Abraham the Intimate Friend of God said:

"My Lord, show me how Thou givest life to the dead," He said, "Dost thou not believe?" He said, "Yes, indeed, but so that my heart may be at peace." He said, "Take four birds and make them be drawn to thee. Then place a piece of them on

every mountain. Then call them: they will come to thee in haste. And know that God is Mighty, Wise."[1]

Note how Moses had certitude about the divine attributes when they are in a state of differentiation (*farq al-ṣifāt*). That is, he directly heard God's attribute of speech, but he wanted to ascend to a direct knowledge of the unity of the Essence. In contrast, Abraham experienced the oneness of the Essence and wanted to descend to know the divine attributes in a state of differentiation.

1 Q Baqara 2:260.

And unto God prostrates whosoever is in the heavens and on the earth, willingly or unwillingly

What is prostration (*sujūd*)?

In the terminology of our Order, prostration denotes the station of complete obliteration of the "I" of dust (*al-anā al-turābī*) in the "He" of Light (*al-huwa al-nūrānī*). It is the supreme act of withdrawal from all-things-other-than-God (*tajrīd*), insofar as it obliterates the lower human nature, so that your essence becomes effaced in the exalted Essence of the Lord.

Outwardly, prostration is a form of self-abasement, a display of true servanthood towards the Patron, and a declaration of total submission to the Worshipped One. It is for this reason that prostration is the final position of the prayer, which itself is the link between the temporality of the servant and the eternity of the Lord. The Beloved Prophet ﷺ alluded to this station by saying, "The nearest a servant is to his Lord is when he prostrates, so make supplications abundantly [in this state]."[1]

Nearness to God is not a matter of spatial distance. Rather, His nearness to you means that your existence ceases to exist before His Existence, for He is utterly independent of all partnership. This hadith thus refutes those who hold that God is

1 Muslim, *Ṣaḥīḥ*, K. al-Ṣalāt, #482.

limited by directionality, or that He is "above" in a literal sense, since prostration is outwardly a downward movement. God says: **prostrate and draw near,**[1] and a tradition relates that the Beloved Prophet ﷺ recited in this very prostration that he was commanded to perform: "I seek refuge in Your pardon from Your punishment, and in Your pleasure from Your displeasure, and in You from You." Through that prayer, God folded the divine acts into the attributes, and the attributes into the Essence, so that his was a prostration of total annihilation (*al-fanāʾ al-kullī*).

As for the average believers, God arranged the standing, bowing, and rising to come before the prostration so that the servant becomes annihilated gradually, first in the acts, then the attributes, then the names, then the Essence.

As far as the simple understanding of prostration is concerned, it is for the servant to throw himself entirely back to the dust that is his root. For the face is the noblest part of the human being, and the nose is a symbol of exaltedness, loftiness, and self-grandeur. The prostration thus buries the symbol of his exaltedness in the dust, so that his lower self does not lead him to the same course Iblīs followed. For this reason, a hadith reports that when the child of Adam prostrates himself, Satan withdraws from him and weeps, and exclaims: "Woe unto me! The child of Adam was commanded to prostrate and he pros

1 Q ʿAlaq 96:19.

trated, so Paradise is his! And I was commanded to prostrate, but I refused, and so Hellfire is mine."[1]

The meaning of *willingly or unwillingly*:

Know, dear disciple, that everything in heaven and earth is in prostration before the presence of the Real, submitting entirely to Him. The outward expressions of unbelief that you see are in fact inward manifestations of faith. Unbelief is the exception, not the root, of existence. The root of all creation is the unswerving and innate disposition (*ḥanafiyya*) towards the One. However, creatures have changed it with respect to its form, not with respect to its root. For the root remains unchanged in them; what changes are the outward forms of associationism towards which people turn.

God says: **Thy Lord decrees that you worship none but Him,**[2] and God's **decree** is firm and does not change. It is not like the predestining (*qadar*) of good and evil. Rather, His **decree** has a single rationale and is a single entity. Thus, there is no object of worship other than God, and whatever His servants turn to in their worship is none other than the Divinity that flows through the various levels of those forms. Each worshipper chooses a certain form, and prefers that form only because of a correspondence that exists between him and it, turning towards it because of the innermost secret by which it subsists.

1 Muslim, *Ṣaḥīḥ*, K. al-Īmān, #81.
2 Q Isrā' 17:23.

God therefore divided prostration into two sorts by saying: **willingly or unwillingly**. The willing prostration is for those who proclaim God's oneness and remain upon the innate disposition of "**Yes Indeed You are our Lord.**" They did not forget their Covenant with their Lord when their spirits were blown into the bodily shadows of existence. The unwilling prostration is for those in whom the innate disposition was altered, so that they were seduced by forms and became attached to the traces of cosmic existence, forgetting their Covenant with God.

How could you then ascribe partners to God, dear disciple, when all separative entities are impossible, and all things other than God are imaginal? Everything is prostrating and proclaiming God's oneness, and the reckoning and recompense concerns intentions alone. Those who are intent on proclaiming God's oneness have been guided to their innate disposition, and those who are intent on pursuing other-than-God will attain the object of their intent.

One of the aphorisms of al-Iskandarī reads, "God was, and there was nothing beside Him; and He is now as He was."[1] Everything in existence is a covering by which God conceals the innermost secret of creation. The manifest dimension of engendered existence is a deception, and its nonmanifest dimension is a lesson to behold; although at a certain level its deception is another of its lessons. The wretched are wretched because of their distance from the root, and the felicitous are felicitous because of their proximity to it.

1 Aphorism #37, Chapter 3. Danner p. 55.

Position (*makāna*) not Place (*makān*)

The so-called hadith of the maidservant[1] has been the subject of extensive scholarly discussion. One group has even used this hadith to justify the belief that God is spatially located in Heaven (*al-samāʾ*). Conflicts over this hadith have resulted in the spilling of much ink. What is even stranger is that in our age when the vastness of space is on full display for the eyes of both the believer and the unbeliever to behold, there are still scholars who talk about the heaven in the same manner as those of the days of old.

God says: **Truly those who deny Our signs and wax arrogant against them, the gates of Heaven shall not be opened for them, nor shall they enter the Garden till the camel pass**

1 Muʿāwiya b. al-Ḥakam said: "...I had a maidservant who tended goats by the side of Uḥud and Jawwāniyya. One day I happened to pass that way and found that a wolf had taken a goat from her flock. I am after all but a child of Adam, and I feel regret just as they do, so I gave her a slap. Then I came to God's Messenger and felt that I had done something grievous. I said: 'O Messenger of God, should I not grant her freedom?' The Holy Prophet said: 'Bring her to me.' So I brought her to him. He said to her: 'Where is God?' She said: 'He is in Heaven (*fi'l-samāʾ*).' He said: 'Who am I?' She said: 'You are the Messenger of God.' He said: 'Grant her freedom, she is a believing woman.'" Muslim, *Ṣaḥīḥ*, K. al-Masājid wa-mawāḍiʿ al-ṣalāt, #537.

through the eye of the needle.[1] A hadith describes the gates of Heaven as closing in front of the spirit of the unbeliever.

Where, then, is Heaven?

Know, may God grant you success, that heaven and earth occupy a single locus according to the people of unveiling and certainty, because for them, everything other-than-God is sheer imagination. Now even though this imagined realm appears to occupy space, it has no actual existence. A single place can contain not only a world, but multiple worlds within the same spatial boundaries and without them interpenetrating.

Behold, may God have mercy on you, the meticulous perfection of the Lord. Behold how in **the Work of God, Who perfects all things,**[2] multiple worlds and creatures exist, yet neither overtakes the other: roaming angels, flying jinn, and walking humans—each in their own world.

Now in order to pass from earth to heaven, you do not need to fly upward nor descend downward. Instead, what you need is a luminous spiritual capacity (*quwwa rūḥāniyya nūrāniyya*) that can pierce through the veils. It is in the measure of your luminosity and capacity that you climb and ascend.

An important remark concerning the realms of the unseen and the visible is in order. The earth that you walk upon, dear disciple, is the visible realm. The first heaven, in your case, is the unseen realm. It and all its inhabitants, angels and other-

1 Q Aʿrāf 7:40.
2 Q Naml 27:88.

wise, are unseen for you. But when you pierce through the veil of heedlessness that is cast over the eye of your heart, and the celestial steed of invocation (*burāq al-dhikr*) leads you to ascend to the first heaven, you will find yourself standing on an earth that is different from ours, yet nonetheless an earth with regard to your essence. At that moment, what was once unseen for you will become visible, and what was once heaven will become your earth. The same applies from the first to the seventh heaven.

To this effect, ʿAbd Allāh b. ʿAbbās said: "A solar eclipse occurred during the lifetime of God's Messenger ﷺ, and so he performed the eclipse prayer. His companions asked, 'O Messenger of God, we saw you reaching out for something while standing in prayer, and then we saw you withdrawing.' The Prophet ﷺ said, 'I was shown Paradise, and reached towards a cluster of fruit from it. Had I taken it, you would have eaten from it as long as the world remained.'"[1]

Now when the holy Prophet ﷺ extended his noble hand to pick from the fruits of Paradise, was he in the Garden or on the earth? The congregants behind God's Messenger were seeing him in the prayer niche of his noble mosque in the radiant city of Medina. Yet at the same instant, he was in the celestial Gardens, because he pierced through the veils of the visible world and, by virtue of his intense luminosity, he became unseen with respect to the veiled persons behind him. God describes this by

1 Bukhārī, *Ṣaḥīḥ*, K. al-Adhān, #709.

saying: **Thou seest them looking upon thee, but they see not.**[1]

It is for this reason that after he ﷺ passed on to the Sublime Companion, he became ontologically situated in a place that is unseen, as he said: "What lies between my grave and my pulpit is one of the meadows of the Garden."[2] Behold how place became position, and how the unseen became visible, by the grace of our master the Messenger of God ﷺ.

There are many hadiths on this subject that make this meaning evident. For instance, it is reported that ʿAlī b. Abī Ṭālib said: "I heard God's Messenger ﷺ say: 'Whoever visits his Muslim brother when he is sick, he walks among the meadows of the Garden till he sits down; and when he sits, he is covered with mercy. If it is morning, seventy thousand angels will send blessings upon him till the evening; and if it is evening, seventy thousand angels will send blessings upon him till the morning.'"[3] Thus, the Muslim who visits his sick Muslim brother is walking in the meadows of the Garden by the grace of the Divine Saying, "I was sick, but you did not visit Me."

Now these realities that we are discussing are only understood by the People of Direct Witnessing and Unveiling. As for veiled persons, the highest they can attain is to surrender to what has been said, without figurative interpretation or understanding. If you do understand what we have just explained to

1 Q Aʿrāf 7:198.

2 Aḥmad, *Musnad*, Abī Saʿīd al-Khudrī, #11397.

3 Ibn Māja, *Sunan*, K. al-Janāʾiz, #1432.

you concerning position and place, then by analogy you may draw meaning from the verses of the noble Qur'ān that speak of above-ness (*al-fawq*) and of Heaven (*al-samā'*).

My Mercy Embraces All Things

My Mercy embraces all things. I shall prescribe it for those who are reverent, and give alms, and those who believe in Our signs, those who follow the Messenger, the unlettered Prophet, whom they find inscribed in the Torah and the Gospel that is with them, who enjoins upon them what is right, and forbids them what is wrong, and makes good things lawful for them, and forbids them bad things, and relieves them of their burden and the shackles that were upon them. Thus those who believe in him, honor him, help him, and follow the Light that has been sent down with him; it is they who shall prosper.[1]

God's mercy embraces "thing-ness" itself, for it embraces every particle of engendered existence. It is the existentiating mercy of His sheer bounty and gratuitous favor upon these worlds which were once submerged in the ocean of nonexistence, calling out for help in the silent language of their state. It is a mercy of replenishment from Him to these worlds, so that they may be sustained by Him, from Him, and for Him, and so that the subtle graces of pure meaning may flow through them.

1 Q A'rāf 7:156-57.

His mercy is that innermost secret which flows through the All and within the All, till it became hidden by the intensity of its own manifestation. It is that pure meaning of the Essence, manifest in the attributes of existence, and concealed by them and within them. It is that downward flow of His presence in the levels of existence, by the benevolent Kāf of "*Ka-annaka tarāhu*, as if you see Him." God's mercy embraces everything because it *is* everything, yet it is not a thing, because **nothing is as His like.** God ascribes it to Himself by the possessive pronoun, whose role is similar to the role of the possessive pronoun in the verse: **I breathed into him of My Spirit** (*rūḥī*).[1] God ascribes the spirit to His own Essence because it is the presence that embraces the multiplicity of the names and the variety of the attributes. It is therefore like the breath that flows through the body of the universe. Through it all existent things, which are its bodily members, subsist; and through it existence expresses its own existence, and justifies its existence over its nonexistence.

Now in order to understand the meaning of this mercy which embraces all things, you must first know the name the All-Merciful (*al-Raḥmān*), and understand the difference between it and the name the Ever-Merciful (*al-Raḥīm*), then the secret of these two names in the basmala formula: **In the name of God, the All-Merciful, the Ever-Merciful.**

1 Q Ḥijr 15:29.

Know, may God grant you success, that the name the All-Merciful (*al-Raḥmān*) contains great secrets and eternal Lights. It is the king and master of the most beautiful names, which is why God juxtaposes it with the name of His Essence, Allāh: **Say: call upon Allāh, or call upon the All-Merciful.**[1] His All-Mercifulness embraces all things, and just as the name the All-Merciful discloses itself in the Garden, it also discloses itself in the Fire to the same extent and with the same intensity. God quotes Abraham as saying to his father: **O my father! Truly I fear that a punishment from the All-Merciful will befall you, such that you will become a friend of Satan.**[2]

As for the Ever-Merciful (*al-Raḥīm*), it refers to a gratuitous gift of mercy which He bestows exclusively upon the believers among His creation. So All-Mercifulness is all-encompassing, while Ever-Mercifulness is exclusive, and the basmala is both inclusive and exclusive. It is a dot that hid itself from nonmanifestation, and when it wanted to manifest, it ascended to the letter Nūn of *al-Raḥmān*, and thus showed mercy to everything, because it is everything. Then it came down to the world of revealed Laws and divided itself among believers and non-believers, proximity and distance.

Thus, His mercy embraces all things only because it flows through all things; and it only manifested all things because it subsists in all things, and is manifest through all things. His mercy precedes His wrath, thus embracing wrath itself. For

1 Q Isrā' 17:110.
2 Q Maryam 19:45.

wrath is a disclosure of His mercy, and there is nothing in existence except His beauty. As for His majesty, it is from Him and to Him; and what you suppose to be divine majesty is only a disclosure of the majesty of beauty, not the essence of majesty, which would be beyond the capacity of engendered creation to withstand.

You should also know, may God have mercy on you, that you will not directly taste His mercy that embraces all things until you embrace all things in your heart. Only then will the laws of His wisdom become unveiled to you, and will you see how His mercy encompasses all creation, flowing through each particle and giving each existent thing its due in accordance with its preparedness.

Vying for increase distracts you

You should know, may God have mercy on you, that forgetfulness of God originates from the multiplicity of separation.[1] This multiplicity stems from a vision of imagined fantasies reflected in differentiated forms, names, and properties that suggest a multiplicity of autonomous entities. For each container discloses itself as a distinct reflection within the eye, and leaves a subtle trace in the mirror of the heart. Each time one looks at things with the eye of heedlessness, one increases in distance from what is truly real. When these dots accumulate over the mirror of the heart and become opaque, they mask the innate disposition toward unity upon which God created His creatures, and the darkness of sensory vessels becomes rooted till the heart takes pleasure in them and finds intimacy in them. Then, with the passing of time, the heart denies its luminous origin and becomes blackened and hardened. God says: **But with the passing of time, their hearts became hardened, and many of them are iniquitous.**[2]

The holy Prophet ﷺ said in a hadith: "Temptations will be displayed before the heart just as reed mats are plaited, strip by

1 God being One, separation from Him implies separation from Oneness, hence multiplicity.

2 Q Ḥadīd 57:16.

strip. Whichever heart imbibes them will be marked by a black dot, and whichever heart rejects them will be marked by white dot. Thus, there will be two hearts: one white as a white stone, unharmed by temptations as long as the heavens and the earth remain; and another black and dust-colored like a turbid vessel, neither recognizing good nor rejecting evil, consumed only by its passions."[1]

The temptations of the imagination manifest as nonexistent shapes in the realm of possibilities. It is these temptations that manifest in the loci of separation in the field of vision, and they are what the Prophet ﷺ likened to strips of a reed mat. Every strip is one of the manifestations of separation, which is the cause of forgetfulness among the average believers. Whoever notices the strips will remain where the strips are. He will be seduced by the variety of colors in the strips, and by whether they are long or short, bent or straight. His life will be spent moving from one manifestation to another, without realizing that if the beauty of the strips were removed, he would find them to be identical as if they were a single strip changing from shape to shape, and from color to color.

However, if he were to behold the reed mat as a whole, then through the beauty of the artisanry he would experience the beauty of the Artisan; and through its meticulous arrangement he would behold the marvelous innovation of the Artisan; and through its grandeur he would behold the all-embracing vast-

1 Muslim, *Ṣaḥīḥ*, K. al-Īmān, #211.

ness of the Artisan. He would then become oblivious to the artisanry out of love for the Artisan. The one who is able to behold the whole sees everything from the perspective of Oneness, and beholds the Divine through the unity of witnessing (*waḥdat al-shuhūd*). The autonomous entities and levels of existence look the same to him, for he is submerged in the ocean of unity where each drop is identical with the other. Thus he knows the ocean by knowing the drop.

This is what al-Khiḍr alluded to when he told Moses the Confidant of God, "Your share of my knowledge is like a bird's share of the ocean when it dips its beak." The ocean symbolizes knowledge of the essence of reality, while the bird is the spirit. **[For] every man We have fastened his omen [lit. bird] upon his neck, and We shall bring it forth for him on the Day of Resurrection as a book he will meet wide open.**[1] The **bird**

1 Q Isrā' 17:13. The word *tā'ir* literally signifies a "bird" or, more properly, a "flying creature." Since the pre-Islamic Arabs often endeavored to establish a good or bad omen and, in general, to foretell the future from the manner and direction in which birds would fly, the term tā'ir came to be tropically used in the sense of "fortune," both good and evil, or "destiny." (Asad). "*Omen* here translates *ṭā'irah,* a word that derives from the same root as that for "birds" (*ṭayr*), since the early Arabs, like certain other premodern societies, considered the movement and behavior of birds as indicators of impending good or bad fortune or as harbingers of the positive or negative consequences of a decision or action (R). That God has **fastened** a human being's **omen upon his neck** is an image used to convey the idea that God has foreknowledge of a human being's ultimate destiny and that from this perspective one's destiny is as if sealed about one's neck. The neck is singled out in particular, as it is said to be the site where tokens of either honor or shame are hung— for example, necklaces indicating high social status or honor, or chains or collars indicating servitude (R, Ṭ). Many commentators consider the *omen* upon one's neck to represent

(*ṭāʾir*) takes from the ocean with his beak, specifically by dipping his beak. That dipping is the station of the descent of the spirit to the levels of the lower self in order to inspire in it a desire to seek knowledge. For the resolve of the spirit is extinguished since it pertains to the command of the Lord (*amr rubūbī*), while the drop is a manifestation of union in separation. Thus, the average believers are **distracted by desire for worldly increase.** They are seduced by the vastness of the ocean and are overcome by impotence with regard to knowledge. As for the People of Spiritual Excellence, they draw the water with the bird of their spirits from the ocean of the Essence, and experience the coolness of the plunge. From the separation of the drop, they attain knowledge of the all-comprehensiveness of the ocean. They give everything its rightful due, and observe courtesy in separation and union, for they see union in separation and separation in union, and they say just as the Chosen One ﷺ said: "You are just as You have praised Yourself."

Do not be dazzled, then, by the multiplicity of separation. Return from numbers to the One, and return from letters to the straightness of the Alif (ا), and return from created beings to the Being-Giver (*mukawwin*). Obliterate the all with the Light of the Creator of the all, so that nothing remains but His Light in the heavens and the earth. At that point, return to the realm of

---

one's deeds in life, which, like an omen, portend either bliss or wretchedness in the Hereafter (IK, Q, Ṭ, Z). But many of these same commentators also take it as referring to the Divine Decree, or *qadar* ("measuring out") for each individual." (*The Study Quran*, pp. 698-99).

separation without forgetting union, and you will see a wondrous secret, and behold something beyond expression. That is what is called the Innermost Secret (*al-sirr*).

Let this be the yardstick by which you measure things when you are incapable of discernment. When you find that verbal expression encompasses the subtle allusion, then know that you are still encompassed by the Innermost Secret. However, when you are incapable of speech, your tongue is reduced to silence, and tears run down and burn your cheek, then know that you are approaching the disclosure-site of the Innermost Secret.

The Worlds

The meaning of the physical world (*'ālam al-mulk*, lit. the world of the kingdom) in the terminology of the Karkariyya order:

The world of the kingdom is the visible world in which supra-sensory reality becomes solidified by the human substance. As a result, the shadows of existence which are perceived by the senses become manifest, so that the attribute that is represented by the divine act may be witnessed.

The meaning of the spiritual world (*'ālam al-malakūt*, lit. the world of dominion) in the terminology of the Karkariyya order:

The spiritual world is the world of supra-sensory realities and Lights that is witnessed by inward vision and perceived by the inmost awareness. It is the nonmanifest realm of existence, and the unseen aspect of every existent, where the bodies of the isthmus, the subtle forms, and the individual souls roam. It is thus the reality that flows through every cleft of the world of possibility.

The meaning of the world of invincibility (*ʿālam al-jabarūt*) in the terminology of the Karkariyya order:

The World of Invincibility is the ocean of existence that becomes manifest by the waves of the realm of possibility. It lies outside the encompassment of the attribute of being, and compels relations and entities by the oneness of intimacy, and the veil of overwhelming power which demarcates the unseen from the visible.

Know, may God open your inward vision, that the wisdom behind the creation of the worlds is for manifestation in nonmanifestation, and nonmanifestation in manifestation. For direct knowledge of God is a liminal state between opposites; He is not known directly except by those who are liminal in inward vision, and who combine the knowledge of the two seas and the innermost secret of the two bows' length.

The Real has made these worlds as circles that revolve around the innermost secret of the cosmos, which is the human being. Given that there are diverse means of perception and aspirations, the worlds were established in a manner that accommodates all creatures, that they may find them inhabitable.

The human being is a combination of clay and an inblown breath, a body and a spirit. He is a composite that brings together two opposites, and it is for this reason that the Lord singled the human being out for vicegerency, and bequeathed him with a great trust. But when the darkness of his clay overwhelms the Light of his spirit, he inclines to the physical world and finds solace in it. As a result, the darkness of the containers leave an imprint upon the mirror of his heart to the point that he denies the existence of the Light and supposes it to be an abstract concept with no actual existence. Thus he descends to the **lowest of the low.**[1] As for the one whose light of spirit overwhelms his darkness of clay, he ascends to the spiritual world and is restored to **the most beautiful stature.**[2]

All of this is in keeping with the pre-eternal decree when God cast His Light upon creation. When someone gains from that divine Light, you find them to be constantly searching and longing for his luminous origin and innate, pure disposition. When someone does not gain from that Light, you find him to be constantly fleeing from it, distancing himself from God's folk, and viciously fighting against them and opposing them. This is the secret of the Qur'ānic verse: **Say, 'Each acts according to his disposition'.**[3]

Moreover, you should know, dear seeker, that the worlds are attributes and levels of the reality of the Essence. They are mere descriptions, not multiple faces of the Essence; for there is only one Face. The multiplicity of the cosmic levels is a relative attribution to the existence of the Real, without any division in His Essence. Far be it for Him! They are none other than attributes by which He manifests, so as to make Himself known to His servants.

1 Q Tīn 95:5.
2 Q Tīn 95:4.
3 Q Isrā' 17:84.

Thus, the secret of the physical world is the knowledge of certainty (*ʿilm al-yaqīn*); knowledge in the sense of the Light of the Real that manifests in the heavens and the earths. As for the spiritual world, its secret is the eye of certainty (*ʿayn al-yaqīn*); that is, witnessing that Light and how engendered things manifest by it, and how they are similar in their essences and distinct in their forms. As for the World of Invincibility, its secret is the truth of certainty (*ḥaqq al-yaqīn*), which is the root of the act of engendering.

Now the relation of these worlds to the innermost secret is that they are the locus for understanding the levels of this secret. Thus, in order for you to perfect your understanding of it, you must behold the world with the eye of unity. As long as you inhabit one world to the exclusion of another, your understanding remains deficient. The knower of God is thus the one who inhabits all of them at the same time and in the present moment, and this is only realized by the one for whom time and space have come to nought. He sees a form in the physical world, its luminous attribute in the spiritual world, and its root in the world of invincibility. This triad manifests the secret of **nothing is as His like** upon beholding the thing.

By understanding these worlds, you will understand the meaning of the Prophet's nocturnal journey and ascent (*al-isrāʾ waʾl-miʿrāj*). You will know that journeying is not through distances but through parting veils. If you were to understand the innermost secret of the dot [under the Bāʾ ب], then you would go wherever you wish and whenever you wish. However, the common believers fail to understand this reality, and suppose that the spiritual world is outer space and the planets. God says: **Thus did We show Abraham the spiritual dominion of the heavens and the earth.**[1] Now was that the first time that God's Intimate Friend saw the sun and moon? Surely not! For he did not see the sun and moon of the physical world, but rather those of the spiritual world. For whatever the sensory eye sees is called physical, no matter how far away it is; and whatever the eye of the heart—or the inward eye—sees is called spiritual; and whatever the spirit sees is called invincibility.

To this effect, al-Iskandarī says in an aphorism: "He has permitted you to behold what is **within** engendered things, but He has not allowed you to stop at the selfsame creatures. He says: **Behold what is within the heavens and the earth**, thus opening up the door of instruction for you. But He did not say, "behold the heavens," so as not to direct you towards the mere existence of corporeal bodies."[2]

Thus, engendered things were brought into existence so that you may see the Real within them—in the manner of lovers extinguished in the vision of the Beloved, not in the manner of any heretical notion of unification with God. The one for whom the veil of the physical world is not lifted will not discover the Lights of the spiritual world, just as the one who is not extinguished in the Lights of the spiritual world will not discover the realities of invincibility. For these worlds were brought into

1 Q An'ām 7:75.

2 Iskandarī, *Ḥikam*, Chapter 14, #140; Danner pp. 81-82.

existence in order for the Real to be known through them, not in order for them to be known in themselves.

The Flow (*al-sarayān*)

You should know, dear seeker of truth, that the flow (*sarayān*) is the innermost secret of "where." That is, the innermost secret by which this world subsists, and through which directions are disclosed. The transcendent meanings are spatially confined to their requisite forms, and the receptacles become manifest through their variation. The flow is thus the all-comprehensive unity that is hallowed beyond color, shape, and quality, and is the innermost secret of every color, shape, and quality.

At its root, the flow is the blessed Olive Tree that God describes as being **neither of the east, nor of the west**—that is, it has no direction—and from which is **kindled** the Light of God. It has an attachment to all things, but nothing is attached to it. It flows through all things without conjunction or disjunction. It is the center of the circles of engendered beings, and it possesses everlasting existence. Out of its loving movement toward manifestation, the all-encompassing periphery (*iḥāṭa*) became demarcated, and thus existence manifested in nonexistence, and eternity in noneternity, without any duality.

You should also know, dear disciple, that the flow consists of multiple levels. The flow of the innermost secret becomes manifest through the divine name Allāh, and the divine name Allāh flows through all His beautiful names, and His names flow through His attributes, and His attributes through His acts, and His acts through His properties, and His properties through His engendered phenomena. The flow is thus the reality that sustains this world, and it is referred to as Divinity (*lāhūt*). Thus it is a descent to the locus of manifestation in the realm of possibility that embraces you, though you do not embrace it; and that carries you, though you do not carry it.

The flow is the Kāf of "*as if* you see Him" (*ka-annaka tarāhu*). It has a center and a periphery. Its center is the Perfect Human Being, and its periphery in the realm of possibility is the phenomenal worlds. Or, one could say that its center is the Olive Tree, and its periphery the niche (*mishkāt*), the lamp (*miṣbāḥ*), and the glass (*zujāja*).

The flow is the innermost secret of the wayfarer, and the manifestation-site of God, whom **nothing is as His like,**[1] by means of which you may see Him. It is the trace of the innermost secret, and its mantle. Through it God manifests in the world, and through it He is veiled from the world. It cannot be drawn out, but only glimpsed with awe.

If the seeker has lofty aspirations, clear intentions, and an understanding that goes beyond the outward traces, the flow will be uncovered for him, and he will at last comprehend the meaning of: **Wheresoever you turn, there is the Face of God, and All things perish, save His Face.**[2]

1 Q Shūrā 11.

2 Q Qaṣaṣ 28:88.

The flow is that Primordial Cloud of the Breath of the All-Merciful that embraces the multiplicity of the names and attributes and their traces, and thus brings them forth from nonexistence into existence. It is a presence that sustains the forms in the same way as water sustains the tree; the water is one without plurality, yet the blossoms are of many colors. Similarly, the flow is one, while existent things are of many varieties. The flow is the uncompounded spirit of engendered existence. It is the underlying substance of the forms whose accidental qualities undergo change. The engendered forms are therefore the manifestation-sites, characteristics, and properties of the flow.

II – The Innermost Secret of the Innermost Secret (*sirr al-sirr*)

The Lām of Passionate Love (*lām al-ʿishq*)

Truly I am God, there is no god but I. So worship Me, and perform the prayer for the remembrance of Me.

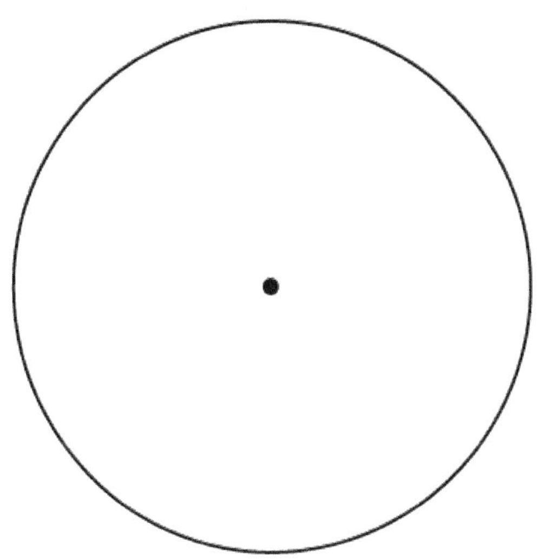

Vicegerency (*khilāfa*)

You should know, dear seeker, that vicegerency is divided into two sorts: an outer vicegerency, and an inner vicegerency. Outer vicegerency [caliphate or political jurisdiction] is well-known and witnessed by all people. Inner vicegerency, however, is hidden from most people because it is generated and realized by the names of the Real. Moreover, some vicegerents combine both outer and inner vicegerency, such as our masters David and Solomon, peace be upon them.

Inner vicegerency constitutes the allegiance of the cosmos to the one whom God makes, in his essence, a realizer of the names of the Real. Such is the one whose form combines the two bows. He is like the basmala of existence, without whom existence would be cut off. For the holy Prophet ﷺ said, "Every important matter that does not begin with the basmala is cut off."[1] He is the center of the cosmos, and all things revolve in his orbit. All things are forms derived from his form, and all spirits are branches of his spirit. He possesses the Staff of the Alif, the Crown of Gnosis, the Seal of the Lām of Contraction, and the Mantle of the Hā' of Identity.

1 Ibn Mājah, *Sunan*, K. al-Nikāḥ, #1894.

Common people typically understand vicegerency to mean the enforcement of penal law, outer rulership, and ensuring that the nation flourishes. This understanding, however, falls short of the totality of vicegerency, because this type of vicegerency pertains to the station of submission (*maqām al-Islām*); or you could call it vicegerency of the divine acts (*khilāfat al-afʿāl*).

However, vicegerency at the station of spiritual excellence (*maqām al-iḥsān*) is the fountainhead of faith (*īmān*) and submission (*islām*). For God's vicegerency on earth occurs when the lordship of your higher spirit rules over the earth of your lower body, so that your spirit has dominion over your body and you rule over it according to God's revealed Law, such that your bodily parts act with faith and subservience to their Lord.

Thus, your body is your kingdom, the heart is the king, and the limbs are its subjects. You must therefore appoint the Light of the Patron as the vicegerent of your heart, then establish its rule over the subjects of your limbs, because it is the reality of God's unswerving revealed Law. God says: **A Messenger has indeed come unto you from among your own. Troubled is he by what you suffer, solicitous of you, kind and merciful unto the believers.**[1] That is, the Light of his Identity that is deposited within you is identical with the innate disposition upon which God created all people.

Now when you are at the Station of the Lām of Contraction, you must learn to entirely contract and nestle within the spirit-

1 Q Tawba 9:128.

uality of the Mediator so that it flows through you and shines its Lights upon your body, and its secrets upon your spirit. This contraction occurs through death in the presence of love. It is called the Lām of Contraction because the passionate souls contract before the presence of its pre-eternal beauty, and they nest like birds basking in the gardens of gnostic sciences, and enjoying the tender fruits of celestial realities.

So die in the love of the Mediator by finding repose under his commands, as the tradition says, "die before you die." The deceased victims of the Lām of Contraction are martyrs (*shuhadā'*), because they witness (*shahidū*) his beauty and splendor, and the magnificence of the secrets and Lights that God deposited in his treasuries. So set free the bird of your innermost secret from the neck of your oath of allegiance so that it may roam in his gardens. God says: **And [for] every man We have fastened his omen upon his neck.**[1]

Masrūq reportedly said in an authentic hadith:

We asked 'Abd Allāh about the Qur'ānic verse: **And deem not those slain for the sake of God to be dead. Rather, they are alive with their Lord, provided for.**[2] He replied, 'We actually asked [the holy Prophet] about meaning of this verse, and he responded: "Their spirits live in the bodies of green birds that nest within lamps suspended from the divine throne. They roam freely in the Garden, and nest in these lamps. Their Lord looked upon them and asked: 'Do you desire anything?' They

1 Q Isrā' 17:13.
2 Q Āl 'Imrān 3:169.

replied, 'What more could we desire, when we roam freely in the Garden?' He asked them the same question three times, and when they saw that they would continue to be asked until they answered, they said, 'Lord, we wish that our spirits be returned to our bodies, that we may be slain for Your sake once more.' And when God saw that they had no need, they were left [to their heavenly joy]."[1]

So be a martyr of love in the Lām of Contraction, and become annihilated with passion, that you may open the gardens of the gnostic sciences to the bird of your essential identity, and that your spirit may soar with the green birds of the names to the lamps of proximity, and enjoy the favor of intimate converse with the Lord of the Worlds.

1 Muslim, *Ṣaḥīh*, K. al-Imāra, #1887.

The Servant (*al-ʿAbd*)

The Servant is the reality from which all perfections stem, for all things are hidden in their opposites. Thus, he is the citrus (*al-utrujja*)[1] whose fragrance of unity pours forth upon the hearts of servants. He is the shadow of the master and His manifestation-site, for he is the witnesser and the witnessed. His garment is the Lights of the attributes, for he is the locus of instruction: a form for you to understand forms; a place for you to understand where-ness. As for his reality, he has neither form nor "where."

To know the Servant, one must be a servant of the Servant. God says: **Say, "O My servants who have been prodigal to the detriment of their own souls! Despair not of God's Mercy.**

1 *Al-Utrujja*: A certain fruit, well known, plentiful in the land of the Arabs, but not growing wild, of the species *citrus medica*, or *citron*, of which there are two varieties in Egypt; one of the form of the lemon, but larger, there called *turunj baladī*, the other, ribbed, and called *turunj muṣabbaʿi*. They are citrons of a large size, which have a sweeter peel than others, and are of a size nearly equal to that of a melon. The sour sort allays the lust of women, clears the complexion, and removes the discoloration of the face (*kalaf*) that arises from phlegm; the peel thereof, put among clothes, preserves them from the moth-worm. It is also beneficial as an antidote against the various kinds of poison; the smelling it in times of plague, of pestilence, is beneficial in the highest degree; and jinn do not enter the house in which it is. A reciter of the Qur'an is appropriately likened to it. (Lane).

Truly God forgives all sins. Truly He is the Forgiving, the Merciful.[1] Observe how He ascribes the servants to the Beloved ﷺ, and through him to Himself.

The Servant is an attribute among attributes. Every attribute must of course have its constituents; and the constituents of the Servant are lowliness and weakness. A sound hadith relates,

"O child of Adam, I was sick but you did not visit Me. He will say, 'Lord, how could I visit you when you are the Lord of the worlds?' He will reply, 'Did you not know that my servant so-and-so was sick, but you did not visit him? Did you not know that had you visited him, you would have found Me with him? O child of Adam, I asked you for food, but you did not feed Me.' He will say, 'Lord, how could I feed You when You are the Lord of the worlds?' God will respond, 'Did you not know that My servant so-and-so asked you for food, but you did not give it to him? Did you not know that had you fed him, you would have found that with Me? O child of Adam, I asked you for water, but you did not give me water.' He will say, 'Lord, how could I give You water when You are the Lord of the worlds?' He will say, 'My servant so-and-so asked you for water, but you did not give it to him. Had you given him water, you would have found that with Me.'"[2]

Thus, the Servant is the one who sustains the necessary attributes of the mold, including weakness, illness, and deficiency, and the attributes that oppose his reality such as inca-

1 Q Zumar 39:53.

2 Muslim, *Ṣaḥīḥ*, K. al-Birr wa'l-Ṣila, #4667.

pacity and ignorance. This is in order for the bodily opacity to draw nearer to him; for were his reality to be unveiled, it would be impossible to draw near to him or take from him.

God says: **Glory be to Him Who carried His Servant by night from the Sacred Mosque to the Farthest Mosque, whose precincts We have blessed, that We might show him some of Our signs. Truly He is the Hearer, the Seer.**[1]

Note that He says, **His servant**, not "His Prophet" or "His Messenger." Note also that the verse begins with **Glory be to Him** (*subḥān*), a proclamation of divine transcendence, lest you imagine any duality. This, that you may know that Servant is the title of the one who was taken on the night journey from the **Sacred Mosque**, which is the locus of manifestation (*majlā al-ẓuhūr*), to the **Farthest Mosque**, which is the locus of non-manifestation (*majlā al-buṭūn*). For it is the Servant who fully encompasses, by the elements of his bodily frame, the entirety of the names. The central point of his essence is the gathering of the Two Bows (*jamʿ al-qawsayn*), and the manifestation of the two opposites. Thus, he is the one addressed by God in His exclusive singularity when He proclaims: **Say** (*qul*). For the Servant is the being that becomes determined as a distinct entity from the divine presence, within the realm of possibility. He is the beginningless Light that displays itself through the form of the human substance that gathers together all principial realities (*ummahāt al-ḥaqāʾiq*).

1 Q Isrāʾ 17:1.

You should also know, dear seeker of truth, that the servant that is alluded to in the Holy Saying as "My servant so-and-so" is the one that is meant here, and not all servants. For all existent and nonexistent beings within the realms of necessity and possibility are God's servants, whereas this specific "servant so-and-so" (*al-ʿabd fulān*) is singled out in himself and for himself. For the Servant is the very center of the resemblant (*mutamāthila*) focal points on the circumference of the Hāʾ of Identity. Indeed, he is the Identity of all things, and were it not for his centrality, the circumference would not manifest. He is thus the fountainhead of the cosmic levels of existence in their undifferentiated and differentiated totality.

A tradition says: "God's most beloved name is ʿAbd Allāh, the servant of God."[1] For it is the manifest and nonmanifest name, and the gathering place of opposites. Servanthood seeks lordship; it does not seek divinity. For divinity rejects duality, in contrast to lordship which requires servanthood. From this we know that the signification of "the servant" goes beyond its surface meaning.

Among those to whom God ascribes this lofty attribute in His holy book is our master al-Khiḍr, may God sanctify his secret. God says: **There they found a servant from among Our servants whom We had granted a mercy from Us and whom We had taught knowledge from Our Presence.**[2] Thus, the conditions of the servant are knowledge and mercy. Mercy, moreo-

1 Muslim, *Ṣaḥīḥ*, K. al-Ādāb, #2132.

2 Q Kahf 18:65.

ver, precedes knowledge. When someone's mercy precedes his knowledge, his knowledge is Light, and the mercy within him will embrace all things, just as his heart will embrace things-as-such, whatever they may be.

You should also know that souls cannot bear patiently with the Servant, except those upon whom God has mercy. God inspired al-Khiḍr to say to Moses: **"Did I not say unto thee that thou wouldst not be able to bear patiently with me?"** thus reminding him of how He had said, **Thou shalt not see Me**[1] in the holy valley. None can bear patiently with him except those whose manner of conduct resembles his, and are preceded by God's providential care.

1 This is a reference to Q Aʿrāf 7:143: **And when Moses came to Our appointed meeting and his Lord spoke unto him, he said, "My Lord, show me, that I might look upon Thee." He said, "Thou shalt not see Me; but look upon the mountain: if it remains firm in its place, then thou wilt see Me." And when his Lord manifested Himself to the mountain, He made it crumble to dust, and Moses fell down in a swoon. And when he recovered, he said, "Glory be to Thee! I turn unto Thee in repentance, and I am the first of the believers."**

The Middle Prayer
(*al-ṣalāt al-wusṭā*)

God says in His holy book: **Be mindful of your prayers, and the middle prayer, and stand before God in devout obedience.**[1]

Know, dear seeker of direct knowledge of God, that everything has its root, and every science has its source. Therefore, take knowledge from its spring. For that is its root and source; it is the ocean that encompasses all rivers and streams. It is the pure flowing water, and the Zamzam of life.

This ocean of knowledge brings together each discipline under its own heading. And just as the book of God Almighty has an archetypal "mother" (*umm*), which is the Opening Chapter (*al-fātiḥa*) that is called the "Mother of the Book" (*umm al-kitāb*), for God summarizes therein everything contained in His holy book—likewise, the prayers have their "mother." The "mother of all prayers" is the middle prayer. God calls it the "middle prayer," that is, the center, and it has a circumference. One might illustrate it by a circle with a central point. It is as though the middle prayer were not one the five canonical prayers, and at the same time is identical with them

1 Q Baqara 2:238.

and is their innermost secret. Thus, no prayer is devoid of it, because each prayer draws from it the number of its units (*raka'āt*), times of prayer, and whether it is said silently or aloud.

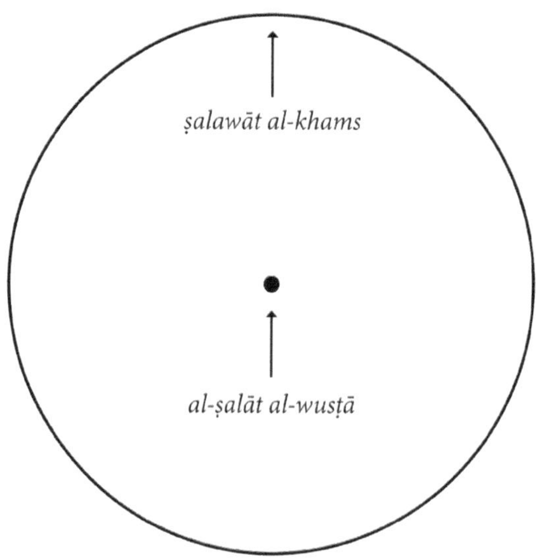

Some scholars define the middle prayer as the late-afternoon prayer (*'aṣr*). They base this on a report related on the authority of 'Ubayda, who stated that 'Alī—may God be pleased with him—reported the blessed Messenger of God ﷺ as saying on the day of the Trench, "They [the unbelievers] prevented us from offering the middle prayer, the *'aṣr* prayer. May God fill their houses and their graves with Hellfire!"[1] It is undoubtedly true that there is a difference between the prayers. For the

1 Abū Dāwūd, *Sunan*, K. al-Ṣalāt, #409.

Beloved ﷺ tells us that the heaviest prayers for the hypocrites are the night prayer (*'ishā'*) and the dawn prayer (*fajr*), saying: "No prayer is heavier upon the hypocrites than the dawn prayer and the night prayer; yet if they knew what was in them, they would attend them even if they had to crawl."[1] In other hadiths, the noble Messenger says: "Whoever prays the two cool prayers (*fajr* and *'aṣr*) will enter the Garden."[2] However, the middle prayer is not any specific prayer, but rather the flow of Light and manifestation-site of the heart-centered connection between the praying subject and the prayed-to Object. It is thus the manifestation-site of the acceptance of the prayer.

From a different perspective, it is the disclosure-site of the Perfect Human Being (*al-insān al-kāmil*) in the realm of worship. It is the door through which a person enters upon his Lord. It is the reverential fear through which prayers are accepted by God. It is the intention that abides in the heart. It is the sheer sincerity (*ikhlāṣ*) that dwells in the deepest recesses of the kernel (*suwaydā' al-lubb*). The middle prayer in its sensory embodiment is thus the blessed Messenger of God ﷺ. In its pure manifestation, it is the perfect heirs who are chosen by the Real to bring forth His servants from the darkness to the Light. That is the true prayer. It is the connection between servant and Lord, eternal and noneternal, existent and nonexistent.

Now in order for you, dear wayfarer in the station of the Lām of Passion, to perform the middle prayer with exacting

1 Bukhārī, *Ṣaḥīḥ*, K. al-Adhān, #657.

2 Muslim, *Ṣaḥīḥ*, K. al-Masājid wa-mawāḍi' al-ṣalāt, #635.

perfection, you must first perfect your ritual ablutions (*wuḍūʾ*) with the water of the unseen (*māʾ al-ghayb*) in the Hāʾ of Identity. This is in order for you to become enveloped in the luminosity of the intermediary in a complete manner. Thereafter, you shall learn how the connection (*ṣila*) flows within the prayers (*ṣalawāt*).

Finally, I conclude this section with a word on the importance of the ritual prayer among the acts of worship. To this effect, a noble hadith reads:

"The first of their deeds for which people will be called to account on the Day of Judgment will be the prayer. Our Lord exalted will say to the angels—though He knows better—'Look into the prayer of My servant, and see whether he has offered it perfectly or imperfectly.' If it was offered perfectly, then it will be recorded for him perfectly. But if it was defective in any way, He will say, 'Look into whether My servant offered any voluntary prayers.' If he offered any voluntary prayers, He will say: 'Complete My servant's obligatory prayer with his voluntary prayer.' Then all the other deeds will be taken into account in this manner."[1]

Furthermore, Muslim relates in his *Ṣaḥīḥ* on the authority of Abū Mālik al-Ḥārith b. ʿĀṣim al-Ashʿarī—may God be pleased with him—that God's Messenger ﷺ said:

"Purity is half of faith. 'All praise belongs to God' (*al-ḥamdulillāh*) fills the scale. 'Glory be to God, and praise be to God'

1 Abū Dāwūd, *Sunan*, K. al-Ṣalāt, #864.

(*subḥān Allāh waʾl-ḥamdulillāh*) fills that which is between the heavens and earth. The prayer is a Light. Charity is a demonstrable proof. Patient restraint (*ṣabr*) is a radiance. And the Qurʾān is a proof either for you or against you. Each person starts his day as the vendor of his own soul: he either frees it, or causes its ruin."[1]

The key phrase here is "the prayer is a Light," for that is the reality of the mediating function (*wāsiṭiyyat*) of the prayer. Similarly—and the loftiest description belongs to God—the Shaykh is a flow (*sarayān*) that pervades the manifestation-sites of the disciples. The disciples, for their part, are the outward disclosure of the connection between creation and the Presence, for they acknowledge the truthfulness of God's summons to creation, while the Shaykh in relation to them is like the middle prayer in relation to the five prayers. He is thus the flow through which they replenish the realities of their existence, both quantitatively and temporally.

Now in order for you to be one of these connections (sing. *ṣila*), you must at this station be a disclosure-site of the Shaykh's lamp (*miṣbāḥ*). His Light must disclose itself brilliantly from your heart, as though you are a flower whose nectar is the Light of love for your Shaykh, upon which the bees of the believers may feast.

1 Muslim, *Ṣaḥīḥ*, K. al-Ṭahāra, #223.

The Most Beautiful Stature
(*aḥsan taqwīm*)

God says, **truly We created the human being in the most beautiful stature, then We cast him to the lowest of the low.** [1]

The Perfect, or Complete Human Being (*al-insān al-kāmil*) is the one who is independent within his self in the essential manner that befits his intent. He is the one who truly knows himself and is not restrained by temporality or circumstance. He is complete because he is created in the form of the Real, and has complete knowledge of himself through unveiling (*kashf*), fruitional experience (*dhawq*), direct knowledge (*maʿrifa*), and state (*ḥāl*).

Know, dear disciple, that God has singled out the human form for the status of perfection because the human form is not an existent that was preceded by nonexistence. For whereas the visible cosmos was brought forth from nonexistence into existence, the human being brought together all the realities that were separated within the cosmos. The human form emerged from separative existence (*wujūd farqī*) into all-comprehensive existence (*wujūd jamʿī*), which is an honor that was bestowed upon none other than it. It is for this reason that the human

1 Q Tīn 95:4-5.

heart embraces the divine mounting upon the Throne (*istiwāʾ ilāhī*), or as one tradition puts it: "My earth and my heaven cannot contain Me, but the heart of My believing servant contains Me."[1]

If people only knew the reality of the Perfect Human Being, the inherent mercy that is bestowed upon him, and the attributes that he encompasses, they would come crawling to give their oath of allegiance to him. They would freely give up their precious possessions as well as their souls, preferring him over the herebelow and the hereafter. One glance at his face is enough to transport the servant through all the stations and degrees. And how can one "prostrate to the shank" (*sāq*) when one does not understand God's immanence in His transcendence? To this effect, an authentic hadith reads, "God will disclose Himself to them in the lowest form in which they imagined Him."[2] Thus, whoever knows the Perfect Human Being knows God, and it is only through him that God can be known, nor is there any entry except through his door, nor any annihilation except in his Lights, nor any subsistence except through his secrets. None honors and recognizes his full worth except his Lord. As for his lovers, they are incapable of describing him, so they prefer to remain silent in his beautiful presence.

Indeed, he is the disclosure-site of **the most beautiful stature** that God created with His own Hands. A hadith from the two

1 This purported Holy Saying (*ḥadīth qudsī*) is cited by Ghazālī in the *Iḥyāʾ ʿulūm al-dīn*.

2 Bukhārī, *Ṣaḥīḥ*, K. al-Tafsīr, #4581.

authentic collections of Bukhārī and Muslim reads: "Verily, God created Adam in His form," or in the narration of Imām Aḥmad b. Ḥanbal, "in the form of the All-Merciful" (*'alā ṣurat al-Raḥmān*). He was assigned to guide people to the Real so that the outpouring (*fayḍ*) and replenishment (*madad*) of the Real may reach them. This replenishment is the cause that sustains the cosmos above and below; for it is impossible for the divine replenishment to reach the cosmos directly, since there is no correspondence between eternity (*qidam*) and noneternity (*ḥadath*). The replenishment thus descends through the Shaykh from the attribute of **the most beautiful stature** to flow through the people of heedlessness in the **lowest of the low**—which is you, O dervish (*faqīr*). Yes, you. Do not be surprised, or deem your soul to be greater than that. Yes, for at this station you are in reality the disclosure-site of the **lowest of the low.** And although among the common believers you may appear to be among the advanced seekers and knowers of God, in fact whatever blessings, awe, divine Light, integrity, and states you may exhibit are none other than disclosures of your Shaykh, flowing from the station of **the most beautiful stature** into your heart. Do not, therefore, exchange that certainty of the reality of your lower self for what the common believers might hear about you. The common believers have no knowledge of your inner self; they know only your outward appearance. That is why you must pray for your Shaykh at this station in each prayer and with each deed. Begin your speech and end it with a supplication for him. Show others his gratuitous favor upon you and his superiority over you; for the blessing of knowledge increases when you ascribe it to its folk. Beware of presuming that you have any rightful claim to anything, or that you possess any blessings or any faith, lest you perish and are driven away from the Presence. For the Shaykh's jealousy knows no limits.

God Created Adam in His Image

God says: **And when I have proportioned him and breathed into him of My Spirit, fall down before him prostrating.**[1] The blessed Messenger ﷺ said: "God created Adam in His form, sixty cubits tall. When He created him, He told him: 'Go and greet those angels sitting over there, and listen to how they respond, for it will be your greeting and the greeting of your offspring.' So he said, 'Peace be upon you,' and they responded. 'Peace and God's mercy be upon you,' adding 'and God's mercy.' Everyone who enters the Garden will enter in Adam's form, but humanity has been shrinking ever since, down to this day."[2]

Know, dear disciple, that this divine proportioning (*taswiya*) is the disclosure-site of the levels of separation (*al-marātib al-farqiya*). The inblowing (*nafkha*), for its part, is the disclosure-site of the true reality of union (*al-ḥaqīqa al-ḥaqqiyya al-jamʿiyya*). Now in order to prevent you from becoming confused—if you happen to be a person who is attached to the sensory realm, or if you are overcome by the veils of where-ness—know that the Real created the human being as a miniature prototype of the cosmos. He is the microcosm (*al-kawn*

1 Q Ḥijr 15:29.

2 Related by Bukhārī and Muslim. The wording here is from Bukhārī, *Ṣaḥīḥ*, K. al-Istiʾdhān, #6227.

al-muṣaghghar), just as the cosmos is the macro-anthropos (*al-insān al-kabīr*). It is for this reason that the human being is the final creation, for he brings together everything that is separated in the cosmos. The human being is the index of the cosmic book, and the stitching of the sensory and the suprasensory worlds.[1]

This is why God speaks of the cosmos and the human being in the same breath in the verse: **We shall show them Our signs upon the horizons and within themselves till it becomes clear to them that it is the truth.**[2] That is, nothing discloses itself to you except the manifestation of the Real (*maẓhar al-ḥaqq*). At times it discloses itself to you in a "sewn together" human state, and at times in a "loosened" cosmic state. The Real discloses Itself to you in a state of union (*jamʿ*) and separation (*farq*). The cosmos is separation, Adam is union, and the inblowing is the "all-comprehensive totality (*jamʿ al-jamʿ*)" which is called the Muḥammadan Reality. It is the letter Yā' (ي) in *Rūḥī* (روحي) [the possessive determiner "my" in **My Spirit**][3] by which the relation between us and the Real is affirmed. It was by virtue of this Muḥammadan Reality that Adam was worthy of vicegerency, and that he learned the names. It was to it that the angels fell down in prostration, for they did not prostrate to his mere earthly shadow of existence. God says: **And when I have pro-**

1 The Shaykh here is referring to the verse: **The heavens and the earth were stitched together** (*kānatā ratqan*) **and We unstitched them** (*fa-fataqnāhumā*) (Q Anbiyā' 21:30).

2 Q Fuṣṣilat 41:53.

3 Q Ḥijr 15:29.

portioned him and breathed into him of My Spirit, fall down before him prostrating. The prostration occurred after the inblowing, not before; that is, the prostration was to the Spirit that was blown into Adam.

You should also know, dear disciple, that the form in which Adam was created corresponds exactly to the form of the Real insofar as attributes are concerned; for God allowed Adam to assume His attributes. Thus you may say that the human being sees and hears, or that he is merciful or noble, though these are really attributes of the Lord. Moreover, the hadith states explicitly that the form (*ṣūra*) is God's. What this means is that Adam was created in the form of His Light which pervades the heavens and the earth. For the heavens and the earth are differentiations of His Light, while Adam is a nondifferentiated stitching of that pre-eternal Light, a Light which is the secret of the **Spirit** that was blown into him.

This Light is therefore from the station of spiritual excellence (*maqām al-iḥsān*). It is the letter Kāf of "*as if* you see Him" (*ka-annaka tarāhu*); and at this station, the Shaykh is the disclosure-site of that Kāf. He assumes the characteristics of the name the Friend (*al-Walī*) in the verse: **God is the Friend of those who believe. He brings them out of the darkness into the Light.**[1] He is the Kāf by which the people of his age are brought out from the darkness of doubt into the Light of certainty. His mortal human nature (*bashariyya*) is metaphorical,

1 Q Baqara 2:257.

just as your spirituality (*rūḥāniyya*) is metaphorical. He is sheer subtlety (*laṭāfa*) just as you are a sheer opacity (*kathāfa*). For this reason, at this station you must exert yourself to become a part of his subtlety, his disclosure-site, and a name from among the names by which he descends into the sensory realm. The blessed Messenger of God once told a man who asked him for advice: "I advise you to feel ashamed before God just as you feel ashamed before a righteous man from your people."[1] So understand!

1 Ṭabarānī, *al-Muʿjam al-kabīr*, #5539.

As If You See Him
(*ka-annaka tarāh*)

'Umar ibn al-Khaṭṭāb said: "One day when we were with God's Messenger ﷺ, a man with very white clothing and very black hair came up to us. No mark of travel was visible on him, and none of us recognized him. He sat down knee-to-knee with the Prophet ﷺ, placed his hands on his thighs, and said: 'Tell me, Muḥammad, about submission (*islām*).' God's Messenger ﷺ replied, 'Submission is to bear witness that there is no god but God, and that Muḥammad is God's Messenger, and to perform the ritual prayer, pay the alms tax, fast during Ramadan, and make the pilgrimage to the House if you are able to.' The man said, 'You have spoken the truth.' We were surprised at how he questioned him and then confirmed his reply. He said, 'Now tell me about faith (*īmān*).' He replied, 'Faith is to believe in God, His angels, His books, His messengers, and the Last Day, and to believe in the measuring out, both its good and its evil.' The man said again, 'You have spoken the truth. Now tell me about spiritual excellence (*iḥsān*).' He replied, 'Spiritual excellence is to worship God as if you see Him, for even if you see Him not, He sees you.' Then the man said, 'Tell me about the Hour.' The Prophet replied, 'About that, he who is questioned knows no more than the questioner.' The man said,

'Then tell me of its portents.' He replied, 'The slave-girl will give birth to her mistress, and you will see barefoot, naked, destitute shepherds vying with each other in the construction of tall buildings.' Then the man went away. After I had waited a while, the Prophet said to me, 'Do you know who the questioner was, 'Umar?' I replied, 'God and His Messenger know best.' He said, 'He was Gabriel. He came to teach you your religion.'"[1]

The "As if" or Kāf of spiritual excellence (*kāf al-iḥsān*) is one of the dimensions of the Lām of Passionate Love (*lām al-ʿishq*). Through it, the Real made Himself known to His creation in the playing field of divine similitude (*tashbīh*) and the domain of possibility. Expressing Himself on the tongue of the eminent Imām of the divine Presence ﷺ, He said: "It is to worship God as if you see Him."

The Kāf is a particle of similitude (*ḥarf tashbīh*) between one thing and another; yet how can there be any similitude with the One whom **naught is like unto Him** (*laysa ka-mithili shay'*)?[2]

Know, dear seeker of gnosis, that similitude in the presence of the Real is none other than a disclosure-site of His incomparability (*tanzīh*) in the ontological levels of divine measuring (*taqdīr*). The Kāf of "as if you see Him" is the divine Light by which you witness the graces of the Lord in the receptacles of the senses.

1 Muslim, *Ṣaḥīḥ*, K. al-Īmān, #8. Trans. Murata and Chittick, *The Vision of Islam*, p. xxvii, with some modifications.

2 Q Shūrā 42:11. Note again the *ka* in the verse.

This Kāf of Spiritual Excellence unites creation with the Creator, and discloses itself in the presence of the names through the name the Friend (*al-Walī*). God says: **God is the Friend of those who believe. He brings them out of the darkness into the Light.**[1] God is a Friend, and the servant is also a friend, and the point of similarity, which is the secret of the Kāf of Spiritual Excellence, is that He **brings** people **out of the darkness into the Light**. Thus, the friend of God who attains realization of the Kāf of Spiritual Excellence is the one who, by God's permission (*idhn*), can bring people **out of the darkness into the Light.**

The friend of God does not become a friend of God until his hearing and sight become God's hearing and sight, as related in the authentic hadith from the Chosen One ﷺ, "Whoever offends one of My friends, I declare war upon him. My servant does not draw near to Me with anything more beloved to Me than what I have made obligatory upon him; and My servant continues to draw near to me with voluntary deeds until I love him. When I love him, I become his hearing with which he hears, his sight with which he sees, his hand with which he strikes, and his foot with which he walks. Were he to ask of Me, I would surely give him, and were he to seek refuge with Me, I would surely grant him refuge."[2]

The root of the Kāf of Similitude (*kāf al-tashbīh*) is the Lām of Love (*lām al-ʿishq*). Whoever restores it to its root, the hadith "to worship God as if you see Him" will apply to him. For he—I

1 Q Baqara 2:257.
2 Bukhārī, *Ṣaḥīḥ*, K. al-Riqā'iq, #6502.

mean the friend of God—is the Light of the spirit of oneness that God describes in the verse: **O mankind! Reverence your Lord, Who created you from one soul and from it created its mate, and from the two has spread a multitude of men and women.**[1] When his commanding spirit (*rūḥ amriyya*) shines its Light upon a locus, it extinguishes the inhabitant of that locus from himself. This spirit of oneness is, as God describes, **as a niche wherein is a lamp. The lamp is in a glass.**[2]

This station has caused confusion for many seekers who have entered the spiritual Path while lacking a spiritual guide or a proper intention. They failed to grasp the meaning of divine similitude and incomparability, due to the illness of professing God's incomparability intellectually (*al-tanzīh al-ʿaqlī*), an illness which took hold of their intellects and veiled their hearts. To this effect, our Shaykh Sīdī Ibn ʿAlīwa (d. 1934), may God sanctify his secret, once said: "The furthest people from God are those who are most ardent in professing His incomparability."

Most people are veiled by their mortal human nature from the spirit. God describes them in the verse: **Thou seest them looking upon thee, but they see not.**[3] They are veiled by the very thing that exists in order to benefit them. They treat the door of proximity as though it were the locus of distance. For were it not for their mortal human nature, they would have no

1 Q Nisāʾ 4:1.
2 Q Nūr 24:35.
3 Q Aʿrāf 7:198.

access to the Real at all; yet they seek after a transcendent form, though they are entirely mortal humans and temporal creations. God says, **Had We made him an angel, We would have sent him as a man, thus obscuring for them that which they themselves obscure.**[1] Without the correspondence of forms, there could be no receptivity or understanding.

So do not let the mortal human nature of the Shaykh veil you from his spirituality, nor his humility from his exaltedness, nor his poverty from his abundance in God. For the Shaykh is like the Alif in relation to the letters in the domain of speech; he is all of the letters. Do not let the curves of the letters veil you from seeing the Alif, for it is their root and their essence. Be mindful of this, oblige your heart to be in constant surrender to your Shaykh, and know that everything he says and does is through divine permission. Recognize the importance of his speech and comportment, obey faithfully his commands and prohibitions, and you will win his love. And when he loves you, blessings will befall you and the Real will illuminate your heart.

1 Q Anʿām 6:9.

The Center and the Periphery
(*al-markaz wa'l-iḥāṭa*)

The point (*nuqṭa*) is the concealed mystery (*ṭilsam*) of being and the spirit of existence. It is an unqualified reality (*iṭlāq*) that manifests by descending into the realm of delimitation (*taqyīd*). It is a transcendent meaning whose traces are clearly detectable to the senses.

Know, may God grant you success, that the center is identical with the circle and is its very essence. The periphery, for its part, is an attribute that was born of the center when it loved to become known. The center does not require the periphery; it has no need for it because it subsists by itself, and is manifest through its very nonmanifestation. As for the periphery, it requires the center in the fullest sense, for it has no independent existence, and no attribute can subsist without an object to which it is attributed.

Now the secret of the Hā' (*al-sirr al-hā'ī*) is this periphery. You learned about it in the First Reading of the singular name *Allāh* where you saw the circle as a disk. The connection (*waṣl*) of all the points within the circle became manifest to you, and you saw each point within the disk as identical to the other. **No**

disparity dost thou see in the creation of the All-Merciful.[1] That is, you witness that everything is from God, and make no distinction between the periphery and the center by virtue of the connection that you witness between all the points within the circle. You see all the points as though they were a single large point, within which are an infinite number of points. This is the goal that must be attained in order to master the first gathering (*al-jamʿ al-awwal*).[2]

As for the secret of the Lām (*al-sirr al-lāmī*) in the Hāʾ-reading, it is to witness the center, and to witness the other points as none other than illusions of the attributes. The essence of the circle which you once witnessed in the secret of the Hāʾ is none other than a descent. It is not self-subsistent, nor does it exist except through the essence of the center.

The center then becomes completely transcendent such that it becomes your qibla in all your states, both inwardly and outwardly. The points within the disk become a descent of the center, and you witness none other than the center, until the disk returns to being a circle.

Your gaze, dear disciple, should therefore remain fixed upon the center and totally turned toward it. It is a qibla for your heart after you **turned thy face unto the heaven** of the Hāʾ looking for a qibla to turn toward. So turn to it in all your habitual

1 Q Mulk 67:3.

2 In his writings and lectures, the Shaykh often describes assembling the rings of Light (*jamʿ al-ḥalaqat*) during the invocation as the first "gathering," or as a sign of completing of the first Reading of the Name.

and ritual affairs, so that—if you are sincere—you may gradually become extinguished in love. Each time, a state, a meaning, and a world will become unveiled to you with respect to its essence in relation to existence. With this, you will come to know your inmost identity regarding it, and your relation to it.

Bukhārī's *Ṣaḥīḥ* contains the hadith regarding the Pledge of Riḍwān (*bay'at al-riḍwān*), in which the beloved Prophet ﷺ said, pointing to his own hand, "This is the hand of 'Uthmān," then struck his two hands together to make 'Uthmān's pledge in absentia.[1] Such was the rank of 'Uthmān, the Possessor of the Two Lights (*dhu l-nūrayn*).[2] His status in the Prophet's eyes was as the Prophet's own hand. So strive, that you may come to know your essence in relation to his ﷺ, and beware of showing discourtesy in his presence. This way, you will come to have clarity about who you are. This is one of the doors of spiritual opening that we have unveiled for whoever is prepared to strive and struggle.

1 Bukhārī, *Ṣaḥīḥ*, K. Faḍā'il al-Ṣaḥāba, #3495.

2 Uthmān was married to the Prophet's ﷺ daughter Ruqayya and, following her death, he married the Prophet's other daughter Umm Kulthūm, thus having two lights.

I am the Distributer (*anā al-Qāsim*)

The blessed Messenger ﷺ said: "When God wants good for someone, He grants him profound understanding of religion. I am but a distributer, and God is the Giver. This Community will continue to uphold God's command, and those who oppose them will not harm them, till God's command comes to pass."[1]

Know, dear disciple, that the Beloved Prophet ﷺ is the Perfect Human Being. He is the source of this existence, and the innermost secret that flows through every witnessed object (*mashhūd*). Every perfected human being draws from his perfection, and every knower of God is a speck of his beauty. For he is the Light of Lights; the one who attends to the world of the unseen and the visible. The realm of being and all that it contains is configured from his Light.

Jābir b. 'Abd Allāh, may God be pleased with him, said: "I asked the Prophet ﷺ about the first thing that God created. He replied, 'It was the Light of your Prophet, Jābir. God created it, then created within it all that is good, and after that created all things. When He created it, He placed it front of Him in the Station of Proximity for twelve thousand years. Then He divided

1 Bukhārī, *Ṣaḥīḥ*, K. al-'Ilm, #70.

it into four parts. He created the Throne from one part, the Pedestal from another, and the Throne-bearers and attendants of the Pedestal from another. He placed the fourth in the Station of Love for twelve thousand years, then divided it into four parts. He created the Pen from one part, the Tablet from another, and the Garden from another. He placed the fourth part in the Station of Fear for twelve thousand years, then divided it into four parts. He created the angels from one part, the sun from another, and the moon and planets from another. He placed the fourth part in the Station of Hope for twelve thousand years, then divided it into four parts. He created the intellect from one part, knowledge and wisdom from another, and divine success (*tawfīq*) from another. He placed the fourth part in the Station of Shame for twelve thousand years, then looked at it, and the Light began to drip with sweat. From it poured one hundred and twenty-four thousand drops of Light, and from each drop God created the spirit of a Prophet or a Messenger. Then the spirits of the Prophets began to breathe, and God created from their breaths the saints, the felicitous, the martyrs, and all the obedient believers till the Day of Judgment. The Throne and the Pedestal are thus from my Light. The Garden with all its bliss is from my Light. The angels and the seven heavens are from my Light. The spiritual beings (*rūḥāniyyūn*) and the angels are from my Light. The sun, the moon, and the planets are from my Light. Knowledge, forbearance, and divine success are from my Light. The spirits of the Messengers and the Prophets are from my Light. The martyrs and the righteous are products of my Light. Then He created twelve thousand veils, and placed my Light, which is the fourth part, within each veil for one thousand years. These are the veils of honor (*karāma*), felicity (*sa'āda*), awe (*hayba*), mercy (*raḥma*), clemency (*ra'fa*), knowledge (*'ilm*), forbearance (*ḥilm*), dignity (*waqār*), tranquility (*sakīna*), patience (*ṣabr*), certitude (*yaqīn*), and truthfulness (*ṣidq*). That Light is upon the brow of God's servant. Between each veil is one-thousand years. When that Light pierced through the veils, God made it grow upon the earth, such that it lit up everything that lies between the east and the west, like a lamp on a dark night. Then God created Adam from the earth, and instilled that Light in his brow. Then it passed to Seth, and so on from one pure man to the next, one good man to the next, until God passed it to the loins of 'Abd Allāh b. 'Abd al-Muṭṭalib, and from him to the womb of my mother Āmina. Then He brought me forth into this world and appointed me the Master of the Messengers, the Seal of the Prophets, and the Mercy to the Worlds. That was how the creation of your Prophet began, Jābir.'"[1]

He ﷺ is thus the Distributer of the affairs of the unseen inasmuch as he is the Master of One and All, the Tongue of the Scale, the Just Balance between the cosmic levels' rightful claim to the realities of the Named. He gives every rightful claimant its due, both above and below, whether it be a name, an attribute, an act, or a property. All things are overpowered under his

1 See Suyūṭī, *al-Ḥāwī li'l-fatāwī*, vol. 1, p. 323.

exclusive singularity (*qahr aḥadiyyatihi*) at the Station of Union, and all things become manifest through his inclusive oneness (*waḥdāniyya*) at the Station of Separation.

For the divine Essence is an ocean without waves or agitation. Hence the Perfect Human Being came forth from its unseen realm to apportion the cosmic levels according to the will of pre-eternity. He is thus the center of the divine presence. It is obvious that a circle can only be perfectly divided if one draws a line through its center, and that is why the center is the Distributer.

Now the Lām of Passionate Love is the locus of the descent. Your bestowals and disclosures come to you from it. Just as every vision and witnessing that the disciple sees comes from the heart of the Shaykh, the disciple has no ability to swim in the realm of nonqualification. He is constantly tied to the Shaykh, **swimming in an orbit** in which he put him when the disciple pledged his oath of allegiance. That is why, dear disciple, when you recount your disclosures or visions to the Shaykh, you must strive to be as truthful as you possibly can. To this effect, the Prophet ﷺ said in an authentic hadith: "The worst of lies is to pretend to have seen something in a dream which one has not seen."[1] Bukhārī also narrated on the authority of Ibn ʿAbbās that the Prophet ﷺ said, "Whoever claims to have had a dream which he has not had will be obliged to tie two barley seeds into a knot, which he will not be able to do."[2]

1 Bukhārī, *Ṣaḥīḥ*, K. al-Taʿbīr, #1545.

2 Bukhārī, *Ṣaḥīḥ*, K. al-Umūr al-Manhī ʿAnhā, #1544.

All good comes from the presence of your Shaykh. While he bears the weight of divine bestowals (*tanazzulāt*) that you are unable to bear, he is akin to your **mountain** which **crumbled to dust** and caused you to **fall into a swoon.**[1] He carries many burdens for you of which you are unaware, and this is a disclosure-site of his inheritance of the Station of the Distributor. The rays of distribution of the Presence are released from his central point. So have constant gratitude for him, observe proper courtesy toward him, praise him constantly, acknowledge his favors upon you, and be in a state of humble meekness before his presence, so that you may become among those who are loved by him.

1 Q Aʿrāf 7:143 **And when Moses came to Our appointed meeting and his Lord spoke unto him, he said, "My Lord, show me, that I might look upon Thee." He said, "Thou shalt not see Me; but look upon the mountain: if it remains firm in its place, then thou wilt see Me." And when his Lord manifested Himself to the mountain, He made it crumble to dust, and Moses fell down in a swoon. And when he recovered, he said, "Glory be to Thee! I turn unto Thee in repentance, and I am the first of the believers."**

On the Day when the Shank is Laid Bare

God exalted says, **On the Day when the shank (*sāq*) is laid bare and they are called to prostrate, yet are not able.**[1]

Abū Saʿīd, may God be pleased with him, said, "I heard the holy Prophet ﷺ say, 'Our Lord will lay bare His shank,[2] and every believing man and woman will prostrate themselves before Him. But there will remain those who used to prostrate in the world in order to be seen and heard. They will attempt to prostrate themselves, but their backs will become [so stiff that it is] as though they had one vertebra.'"[3]

ʿAbd Allāh b. Masʿūd said, "God will gather mankind on the Day of Resurrection, and a caller will call out: 'O mankind! Would you be pleased for your Lord—who created you, formed you, and provided for you—to assign each and every one of you to whatever they used to worship in the herebelow, to be under

1 Q Qalam 68:42.

2 That is, the "severest Hour." Lit. *kashf al-sāq* "laying bare of the shank" is a Qurʾānic expression derived from the verse **On the Day when the shank is laid bare and they are called to prostrate, yet are not able. The shank is laid bare** (Q Qalam 68:42). It indicates something very serious and severe. When a person wearing traditional Arab clothing engages in a strenuous endeavor (and sometimes in battle), he begins by rolling up his garment in such a fashion that his shank is exposed." Some exegetes say that in this verse it is God Who exposes His own Shank to signal the beginning of the judgment process. *The Study Quran*, p. 1405.

3 Bukhārī, *Ṣaḥīḥ*, K. Tafsīr al-Qurʾān, #4635.

their protection? Would that not be fair for your Lord?' They will reply, 'Yes, indeed!' Then each of you will set out to whatever they befriended in the herebelow. Whatever they once worshipped in the herebelow will appear to them in an imaginal form, such that the satan of Jesus (*shayṭān ʿĪsā*) will appear to those who worshipped Jesus, and the satan of ʿUzayr will appear to those who worshiped ʿUzayr. Even trees, branches, and rocks will appear in their imaginal forms.

"But the People of Islam will remain in their place. The caller will then ask them, 'Why are you not setting off like the rest of mankind?' They will reply, 'We have a Lord, but we have yet to see Him.' He will say, 'And how would you recognize your Lord if you were to see Him?' They will reply, 'There is a sign between us and Him. When we see that sign, we will recognize it.' He will say, 'And what is that sign?' They will reply, 'He lays bare His shank.'

"At that moment, the shank will be laid bare, and all things will fall prostrate toward Him with their backs, but a group will remain whose backs are like the horns of cattle. They will try to prostrate, but will be unable to do so. Then they will be commanded to raise their heads in the measure of their deeds. Some will emit light that is like a mountain in front of them. Others will emit light like palm-trees on their right sides. Some will emit less light. The last one to emit light will emit it from the big toe of his foot, and his light will flicker on and off. When his foot gives off light, he will advance, and when it falls dark he will remain in place.

"Then they will cross over the Bridge (*ṣirāṭ*), which is razor-sharp and perilous. They will be told: 'Save yourselves in the measure of your light.' Some will cross over it like shooting stars, others like the blink of an eye, others like the wind, others like a man stumbling up a sand-dune, each crossing in the measure of their deeds. This will continue till the one who emits light from the big toe of his foot crosses, pulling one hand and clinging with the others, dragging one foot after the other, the Fire drawing close all around him. They will be saved, and once they are saved, they will cry out, 'Praise be to God who delivered us from you, after what He showed us of you! God Almighty has given us what He has not given anyone else!'

The hadith continues, adding that God will say to them, "Would it not please you if I were to give you the equivalent of this lower world from the day I created it till the day I extinguished it, and ten more besides it?"[1]

Know, dear disciple, that the divine Throne (*'arsh*) is the locus of the mounting (*istiwā'*) of the name the All-Merciful. The All-Merciful is called the king of the names because God paired it with the divine name Allāh, and it thus came to occupy the most exalted level and the closest degree. God says: **Say call unto Allāh, or call unto the All-Merciful.**[2] It is by virtue of this that the name the All-Merciful is the ceiling of the names. It has one face toward the unstitched differentiation (*fatq*) of the

1 Dāraquṭnī, *Sunan*, K. al-Ru'yā, #116.
2 Q Isrā' 17:110.

most-beautiful names, and another toward the original undifferentiated stitching (*ratq*) of the supreme name, Allāh.

The Throne is therefore one of the manifestation-sites of the name the All-Merciful. As for the shank, that is, the shank of the throne, it is the Hidden Alif (ا) that flows through the names al-Raḥmān (الرحمن) and Allāh (الله). It is the manifestation-site of divine transcendence in the realm of possibility. It is through it that the Real makes Himself known to His believing servants in the herebelow. For as the abovementioned hadith states, "He will say: 'And how would you recognize your Lord if you were to see Him?' They will reply, 'There is a sign (*ʿalāma*) between us and Him. When we see that sign, we will recognize it.' He will say, 'And what is that sign?' They will reply, 'He lays bare His shank.'"

Note, may God have mercy on you, how the believers have a luminous covenant and a sign in their hearts in this world by which they know the Real. He stored it for them for the Day of Resurrection, so that He may unveil for them its greatest secret and its most magnificent treasure.

The People of God among the Shaykhs who train disciples (*mashāyikh al-tarbiya*) are a locus of manifestation of sanctity (*wilāya*); **no fear shall come upon them, nor shall they grieve.** It is through them that the Real directs His creatures to Him. For they are God's true measuring (*taqdīr*) in the realm of possibility; they are the disclosure-site of the storehouse of knowledge and treasures of gnosis. There is no path except through their door, and no entry except by their permission, and no ascending or descending except by their command. A gaze at them is equal to years of worship. For they are the disclosure-site of the unity of the Presence, and the initiatic tree, and the Light of God, the Patron. They are the Lām of Passionate Love whose affection is addressed to every being: the trees, the stones, the soil, humans, and jinn. If you deny their presence and are hostile toward them, your spirit nonetheless prostrates in humiliation at their feet. Therefore, be obedient **willingly** instead of **unwillingly**. For the form of the friend of God in your age will be your guiding lamp on the Day of Resurrection, your security on the Day of Fear, and your deliverance on the Day of the **Greatest Terror.**[1] It will be your guide on the **day when eyes and hearts will be turned about.**[2] The form of the friend of God in your age will preserve you from stumbling and following the forms of separative entities (*aghyār*) that would sweep you away into the Fire of distance. For his form was, and continues to be, one of the measured determinations of the Presence. It is the firm rope to which whoever holds fast will be guided, and whoever seeks Light from its Light will pass over the Bridge like lightning.

The Lām of Passionate Love is a rope; whoever holds fast to it will win on the Day of Resurrection. They will attain proximity, security, and the vision of the All-Merciful. Whoever rejects it will have no qibla on the Day of Resurrection. They will be unable to prostrate because they are stripped of the affective

1 Q Anbiyā' 21:103.

2 Q Nūr 24:37.

inclination of passion, so they will be unable to bend the Alif of their backs. For in this world they used to be hypocrites; they ridiculed, provoked, and slandered. God tells us what their fate will be on the Day of Resurrection: **On the Day when the hypocrites, men and women, will say to those who believe, "Wait for us that we may borrow from your Light," it will be said, "Turn back and seek a Light!" Thereupon a wall with a gate will be set down between them, the inner side of which contains mercy, and on the outer side of which lies punishment. They will call unto them, "Were we not with you?" They reply, "Indeed! But you tempted yourselves, and hesitated, and doubted; and false hopes deluded you till the Command of God came, and the Deceiver deceived you concerning God.**[1]

1 Q Ḥadīd 57:13-14.

Truly those who pledge allegiance unto thee pledge allegiance only unto God

God says: **Truly those who pledge allegiance unto thee pledge allegiance only unto God. The Hand of God is over their hands. And whosoever reneges, reneges only to his detriment. And whosoever fulfills what He has pledged unto God, He will grant him a great reward.**[1]

A pledge of allegiance to God's folk is a pledge of allegiance to God. It is a pledge that is devoid of intermediaries, though it may be qualified by them. The sign that one has pledged allegiance to the Light of God is the instantaneous illumination of the heart. Your pledge of allegiance to God's folk is preceded by God's invocation of blessings upon you. For God says, **He it is Who blesses you, as do His angels, that He may bring you out of darkness into Light. And He is Merciful unto the believers.**[2] The blessing of being singled out for mercy flows through you, and thus the Light of the Real discloses itself to you in plain sight, and you see it with the eye of the heart in the waking world. Pledging allegiance to the Lām of Passionate Love is a pure pledge to God, wherein the Hand of God is above the hand of the one giving the pledge. It is a basmala whose secrets

1 Q Fatḥ 48:10.
2 Q Aḥzāb 33:43.

flow through the heart of the pledger, upending him so that what was once low is now high, and drawing him closer to the Presence after he was once far from it. The pledge determines the measure of faith in the unseen in his heart, and traces out the orbit wherein it floats. Whoever fulfills what he has pledge shall earn the wage of the verse: **faces that Day shall be radiant, gazing upon their Lord.**[1] The blessed Prophet ﷺ said: "You shall see your Lord in the Hereafter as you see this moon, and you shall not have to strain to see Him."[2] This is a moon you can see in this world before the next, because the Real is not confined to time any more than He is confined to space. Thus, the day of the pledge of allegiance for the People of Light is the beginning of the Day of Increase (*yawm al-mazīd*). God tells us of the discourse of Abraham the Intimate Friend:

Thus did We show Abraham the spiritual dominion of the heavens and the earth, that he might be among those possessing certainty. When the night grew dark upon him, he saw a star. He said, "This is my Lord!" But when it set, he said, "I love not things that set." Then when he saw the moon rising he said, "This is my Lord!" But when it set, he said, "If my Lord does not guide me, I shall surely be among the people who are astray." Then when he saw the sun rising he said, "This is my Lord! This is greater!" But when it set, he said, "O my people! Truly I am quit of the partners you ascribe.[3]

1 Q Qiyāma 75:22-23.

2 Bukhārī, *Ṣaḥīḥ*, K. al-Adhān, #806.

3 Q Anʿām 75-78.

The Intimate Friend saw the Light of the Almighty and said, **This is my Lord**, for he knew that it was the Light of the divine attribute by which the Real disclosed Himself to him. He had no doubt; and far be it for him to doubt. Rather, he described the Light as an attribute of the Lord—in contrast to some who show up at the door of the Presence, and through the Shaykh's gratuitous kindness, make the pledge of allegiance, but then when they see the Light of the Almighty, they fall into doubt and withdraw.

The pledge of allegiance to the Shaykh is a pure pledge of allegiance to God, for it is sheer subtle grace. It is a Light from the Light of the Almighty; a mirror of the attribute of the Real; a lamp that shines brilliantly upon the physical world. Were it not for the glass (*zujāja*) of concealment, its luminosity would burn the eye that beholds it. Thus should you recognize the Lām of Passionate Love: behold it with the eye of lordship; see it just as God described it; treat it in the outer realm with respect and honor, and in the inner realm with worship and sincerity, so that you may stand at the station of courtesy with the presence of God's folk.

III – The Ultimate Innermost Secret (*sirr sirr al-sirr*)

The Lām of Gnosis (*lām al-ma'rifa*)

You did not slay them, but God slew them, and thou threwest not when thou threwest, but God threw.

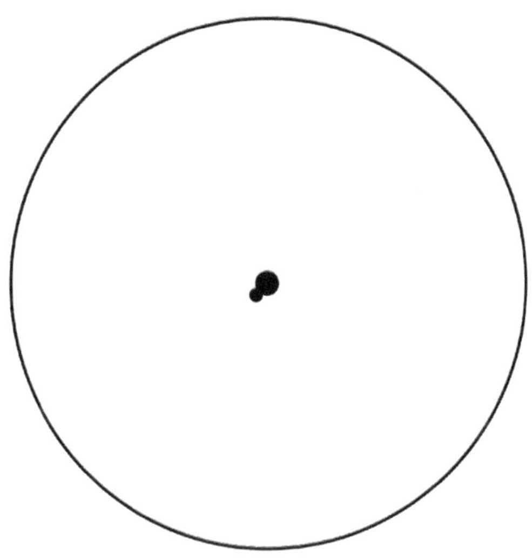

The Shadow

God Almighty says in Sūrat al-Furqān: **Hast thou not considered thy Lord, how He spreads out the shadow—and had He willed, He could have made it still— and then We make the sun an indicator of it, then We withdraw it unto Ourselves, a gentle withdrawal.**[1]

Qushayrī says in the *Subtle Illusions*: "The blessed Messenger ﷺ halted on one of his trips to take a nap under the shadow of a tree. There were many people there, and God spread out the shadow of the tree till it encompassed them all, despite how numerous they were. Then God revealed this verse. This was one of the Prophet's miracles."

And I say:

Is it myself or my shadow that you see?
This can be grasped only by him who has become like me.

Know, dear wayfarer, may God give you insight into the celestial reality, that the tree of sainthood is the source of the shadow under which the locus of the Message sought shade, for the tree of sainthood is the fountainhead. With respect to the Lām of

1 Q Furqān 25:45-46.

Knowledge which we are currently discussing, you must learn how to realize the pure meaning of the shadow so that you may be delivered unto it. Become realized in it, so that you may become a shadow of the Lām of Passionate Love, and be the glass of the lamp of love. With this, the sciences of the lamp will be disclosed from you, as well as its affairs, states, and levels. Thus, the lamp of love will remain hallowed beyond form, and you will become its form in the sensory realm.

The shadow is the locus of the unseen in the visible realm. It is neither existent nor nonexistent. Its role is to give determinations of the rays of "I loved to be known" that shine forth from the sun of reality upon the soul of the vicegerent. Through these determinations one recognizes the descent of the determinations of the prayer of union, and its courtesies and proper times. To this effect, Shushtarī says:

At noon time,
Your secret flows to me.

For noon is the time when the sun reaches the middle of the sky, and this time is known as the time of standing, such that the sun reaches the zenith (*khaṭṭ al-zawāl*), which is an imaginary line that divides the sky into two halves, eastern and western. When the sun reaches the imaginary line of noon, the shadows are at their shortest. For the sun is closest because it is directly above. At this moment, everything contains its shadow within it, so that the shadow is with the essence, and the sun is upon the straightness of the Alif. This is the time of manifestation (*ẓuhūr*). And because the Wāw (و) of extension resides in the Hā' of the circumference, this *ẓuhūr* (ظهور) becomes *ẓuhr* (ظهر midday), and so you perform the prayer of the union of *ẓuhr*.

Every disciple at the station of the Lām of Gnosis is one of the shadows of the determinations of the Shaykh, acting as a guide for the manner in which one connects with the intermediary. This is why you find that the disciples differ in their states, unveilings, and variegations. You find one of them roaming in the angelic world, another in the world of minerals, another in the world of colors, another in the world of letters, and another in the world of numbers. The more their annihilation in, and love for, the reality of the Shaykh deepens, the closer their orbit draws to the Shaykh's celestial body.

God says with regard to Moses, God's Confidant: **So he watered [the flocks] for them [the daughters of Shuʿayb]. Then he withdrew under the shade and said, 'My Lord! Truly I am in need of any good that You may send down upon me.**[1]

Dear wayfarer, emulate the courtesy of Moses, and turn toward the shade under the tree of the pledge of allegiance. Beware of direct exposure to the rays of the sun of divinity, for you have no ability to withstand its rays, which obliterate all appearances of duality. Withdraw to the shade of lordship, for its shade leaves room for servanthood. Cling to humility, and

1 Q Qaṣaṣ 28:24.

regard your lower self with contempt; for whatever spiritual opening you may have attained, it is but a drop in the ocean. Say: **My Lord! Truly I am in need of any good that Thou mayest send down upon me.** Never become satiated of God's bounty, for otherwise your spiritual opening will become a veil onto itself. May the everlasting presence forever remain your highest saintly aspiration.

The Mirror

Know, dear seeker of realization, that the science of the mirror is a wondrous science, and its secret is a unique secret. However, given that we are speaking of the [Lām of Gnosis through the prism of the] Hā' of Identity, we shall only reveal the basic precepts of gnosis that the station permits, so that the reader is not distracted and drawn to what lies behind the unseen realm and the wonders of creation, thereby forgetting the Creator. That is why we only speak about the introductory levels of this science, so that hearts may find comfort and minds may absorb it.

The Lām of Gnosis contains the mirror of your Shaykh, wherein you may see the true reality of yourself. For how far apart are the one who sees himself in his Shaykh, and the one whose Shaykh sees himself in him! At this level of the presence, you learn to be a reflection of your Shaykh when you become absent from yourself. Then you become a firebrand drawn from the reality of the Shaykh, walking among people, and it is in the measure of your realization of the qualities of your Shaykh that you attain sure footing in the Lām of Gnosis.

But beware of thinking that you are the Shaykh or his peer, or of your soul suggesting such a thing to you. Many feet have slipped at this station, especially at the Lām of Gnosis. Those who became obsessed with their lower selves incurred this affliction only because they did not regard their souls with contempt, and did not revere their Shaykh. If only this reverence were to take hold of the heart of the disciple, he would not dare to think of himself as being worthy of assuming the station of his Shaykh. Rather, he would find pleasure in the station of poverty, and make it his heart's homestead.

Anyone thinks that he is worthy of the reflection descends from **the most beautiful stature** to **the lowest of the low.**[1] In so doing, he descends from the Adamic station and vicegerency to the demonic station. According to an authentic tradition, Ṣafiyya bint Ḥuyay, may God be pleased with her, said: "One night I went to visit the Messenger of God ﷺ while he was in a spiritual retreat. I conversed with him for a while, then got up to leave. He got up to give me a kiss, and just then two men of the Helpers passed by. When they saw the Prophet ﷺ, they quickened their pace. He said to them, 'No need to hurry. It is only Ṣafiyya bint Ḥuyayy.' They said, 'Glory be to God, O Messenger of God!' He said, 'Satan flows through man like blood in his veins. I feared that he would cast some wickedness into your hearts, or say something.'"[2]

The devil flowed through Adam's veins, and so when the angels prostrated to him as the devil flowed inside him, the devil thought that he himself was the one to whom they were

1 Q Tīn 95:4-5.

2 Bukhārī, *Ṣaḥīḥ*, K. Bad' al-khalq, #3281; Muslim, *Ṣaḥīḥ*, K. al-Salām, #2175a.

prostrating, and that he was not required to fall down prostrate alongside them. He held himself in reverence because of his worship and proximity, and thought that he was the important one. However, the divine will decreed that he be in the position of lowly servitude while Adam was raised high, and thus Adam became a disciple (*murīd*), while Iblīs became a rebel (*marīd*).

Be extremely cautious of this sort of thing. Be cautious again and again, and imbibe this station slowly. Be astute and mindful, and know that the measure of your realization through your Shaykh at the Lām of Gnosis will be the extent to which you adorn yourself in his noble state. If you ask how this realization is to be achieved, then the Hadith of the Walī is your guide, for when your hearing becomes the hearing of the Shaykh, and your seeing becomes the seeing of the Shaykh, and your hand becomes the hand of the Shaykh, and your foot becomes the foot of the Shaykh, it is then that you will achieve realization of the Lām of Gnosis. The more you assume his traits, the greater your realization will become, and the firmer the signs will be fixed within you.

God says: **Whatever good befalls thee, it is from God, and whatever evil befalls thee, it is from thyself.**[1] The proper etiquette of the disciple at this station is to behold every negligence, appetite, and shortcoming as issuing from himself, and ascribed to himself; and to behold every virtue, pious act, and wakeful moment as a reflection from the mirror of his Shaykh.

1 Q Nisā' 4:79.

With this, he refers the blessing to its rightful owner. He must maintain this until he passes away in his Shaykh completely, and sees in himself none other than his Shaykh. Thereupon, he ascribes everything to the Presence, and no trace of him remains. It is then that the verse truly applies to him: **Say, "All is from God."**[1]

1 Q Nisā' 4:78.

A Span of Time

God says: **Has there come upon man a span of time in which he was a thing unremembered?**[1]

Know, dear wayfarer, that time (*dahr*) is one of the disclosure-sites of divinity. In a Holy Saying, Abū Hurayra, may God be pleased with him, related that the Messenger of God ﷺ said, "God says, 'The child of Adam offends me by insulting time; for I am time. In My hand is the command. I turn the night and the day.'"[2] The span (*ḥīn*), for its part, is a descent to the station of lordship, wherein the existence of the servant may be acknowledged.

Know that in the Lām of Gnosis at the disclosure-site of the Hā' of Identity, the lover becomes the beloved, and the speaker becomes the hearer—without connection or disconnection, but rather through the secret of the Lām of Gnosis, and the secret of the glass that reflects in it all of the lamp's Light, so that everyone thinks that the glass is the light-giver, just as the moon appears to the eye as a bright star, even though its light is none other than a reflection of the light of the sun. So the station of the Lām of Gnosis is the station of complete absorption,

1 Q Insān 76:1.

2 Bukhārī, *Ṣaḥīḥ*, K. al-Tawḥīd, #7491; Muslim, *Ṣaḥīḥ*, K. al-Alfāẓ min al-adab wa-ghayrihā, #2246b.

wherein no noticeable trace of duality persists. It is a single human substance containing two spirits: one spirit for transmission, and another for reception.

For this reason, we began our discussion with the noble verse from Sūrat al-Insān in order to bring the meaning closer to you. For the Shaykh at this station becomes a hidden meaning, accepting neither addition nor duality. Rather, he descends upon the disciple, manifesting in the **span of time**. Indeed, at this precious station you become a descent of the Shaykh; he is the unseen, and you are the visible; he is transcendence and you are immanence; he is the ink and you are the letter. Thereby, if destiny favors you, you become **a thing remembered**, when before you were **a thing**, but a thing that was **unremembered.** You were not remembered within the center of the Divine Presence, but now you are remembered therein, and you exist through Its secret, subsisting through Its Essence. You belong entirely to Him, and part of you has passed away in His Essence. Nothing of you remains for yourself, and you witness of yourself none other than your Shaykh, just as Ibn ʿAbbās, may God be pleased with him, used to look into the mirror and would see the image of God's Messenger ﷺ, not his own image.

You should know, moreover, that the extent of the **span** that one realizes is different from disciple to disciple, for each takes from the Shaykh to the extent of his capacity and his strength. The **span** we are discussing here is the moment of the spiritual opening, of which most of those in the spiritual retreat are barely aware. It is where union and the folding of heaven and earth occur, for each disciple in accordance with the divine preordainment.

Thus, in order to perfect this descent, you must be constantly attentive to the advice of the Shaykh, and to everything he says, even when he seems to be speaking casually. For he does not stray from the truth, because he is protected by God. So observe him in his states and deeds, and emulate them, and do not imagine that in so doing you are contradicting the revealed Law, for what a difference there is between theory and practice of the Law.

He who knows himself

God says: **So when I have proportioned him and breathed into him of My Spirit, fall down before him prostrating.**[1]

Know, dear seeker of truth, that sacred inblown breath was the reason for the prostration of the angels of the supreme assembly. This inblown breath is the Breath of the All-Merciful within the world of elemental bodies which was proportioned in order to receive this reality, from whose core the royal pronoun "We" comes forth. It was through this that the quality of the Essence appeared in existence, and so the Adam of the Names became the qibla for the angels in heaven, and they prostrated before him, just as we prostrate before the noble Kaʿba.

In this manner, the hidden Essence became manifested within the visible realm of the names, just as letters manifest the reality of the soul, disclosing what is hidden in the visible realm. It is worth bringing attention to what is called transcendent incomparability (*tanzīh*) and immanent comparability (*tashbīh*). For God possesses exclusive eternal transcendence, just as He is by Himself and for Himself; but because of love and the principle of making Himself known, He sent to us, from the

1 Q Ḥijr 15:29.

world of the treasure, the breeze of "I loved to be known." That is transcendent immanence (*tashbīh munazzah*), and thus the two opposites became visible, and the truth concealed itself between them.

The right way, for those who wish not to slip, is to bring together immanence and transcendence; for the one who sees with only one eye is a half-blind Dajjāl. The essence of this matter is that the one who recognizes himself through immanence, and brings that back to the reality of transcendence, will behold plainly the innermost secret between them, which is the bridge between the nature of the lower self and the innate disposition of the spirit. That is why it is said that "the one who recognizes his self, recognizes his Lord."

Note that he did not say "recognizes his God," for there is a big difference between the two. For the divine name "Allāh" has no partner with Him: neither servant nor angel, neither existence nor nonexistence; while the name "Lord" implies the master-servant duality. These are the two aspects of the Reality that is concealed due to the intensity of Its manifestation.

Thus, you behold the servant and know the Lord, while divinity is concealed from you either because of the intensity of transcendence or the dictate of immanence, while the divine reality is an isthmus between the two. It is an imaginary line between the existence of the Lord and the shadow of the human being.

The one who wishes to recognize himself must find the believer's mirror, which is the Perfect Human Being, for in his mirror you see your reality that is concealed from you by the imagined directions and multiplicity of perspectives. The one who is led by divine will to a perfect Shaykh must don the garb of satisfaction and surrender for his encounter, so that his soul may be satisfied with being a secondary reflection in the original mirror of his Shaykh. Let him embark upon the vessel of complete impotence in order to traverse the stormy ocean in which many would-be seekers of self-recognition have drowned. For when their souls were unveiled to them, they fled in denial, seeking not divine unity but instead returning to their metaphorical existence, and remaining in duality, the quarry of polytheism—we seek refuge in God from that!

To this effect, Shaykh al-ʿAlawī, may God sanctify his secret, said:

You desire divine unity and seek it from us,
But if we told you what it is, you would flee from us!

Annihilation and Subsistence

Know, dear loved ones, that what veils the disciple from his Lord is his lower self. This is because God does not forgive that a partner be associated with Him, and so long as the disciple sees himself as existing, he is in the veil of distance from the presence, because he makes his existence partner to the existence of the Real, and the presence of oneness does not accept duality, and is beyond partnership. This is why it is necessary for the spiritual wayfarer to pass away from his lower self.

In the terminology of our Order, annihilation (*fanāʾ*) means to be attracted by the magnet of love to the center of the Real, and to come to naught in His Light, until the act disappears in the attribute, and the attribute in the name, and unto the presence of "God was, and there was nothing beside Him."

This annihilation takes place in stages. It begins with repenting from outward acts of disobedience, and holding to this repentance. Then comes shedding the darkness of the lower self, which is the fountainhead of the illusory realm of separation and the center of things, directions, standpoints, and determinations. This can only occur through the Light of the saint that enables others to arrive, for he is the door of the city of subsistence. Thereupon your hearing passes away in his hearing, your seeing in his seeing, your hand in his hand, and your foot in his foot, until you see in yourself none other than your Shaykh, thereby passing away from yourself and subsisting through him, such that you become him. As such, he becomes your luminous transcendence that abides through God's command within you, and you become present with him through constant witnessing of him, by virtue of the subsisting adornment of pure affinity: **Say, "All is from God."**[1] You exist through him within the very realm of separation, and his beauty reflects itself in existence and encompasses all things.

As for subsistence (*baqā'*) in the terminology of our Order, it is the reality that subsists after complete annihilation in the very realm of separation, with neither nonexistence nor existence, neither witness nor witnessed: "and He is now as He was."

The measure of the annihilation determines the measure of the subsistence, just as the measure of self-emptying determines the measure of adornment. God's grace is broader for those whom He loves.

You should know, moreover, that after every annihilation there is subsistence, and after every subsistence there is annihilation. You pass away from one veil, only to subsist in the veil that comes after it, and so on, until you attain complete subsistence beyond which there is no further annihilation. That is the real subsistence that is built on complete annihilation; it is the complete ascension, and the station of the pupil of the eye of existence, the cornerstone, the brick in the wall of the treasury.

1 Q Nisā' 4:78.

The Pronouns

Know, dear wayfarer, that when the disciple sees the flame of spiritual struggle as a Light in his heart and follows it, it guides him gradually to **the holy valley of Ṭuwā.**[1] Then when he discards his sandals there at the Tree of Identity, the Lordly nature of the tree reflects upon his human substance through the secret of God's words: **Truly I am God, there is no god but I,**[2] so he plunges into the ocean of union itself, where there is risk that the waves of the "I" will beguile him.

"I" and "He" are pronouns between which the wayfarer lives, like iron between the hammer and the anvil. For existence does not tolerate for there to be two "I"s. If the disciple were to say it, or to believe it in his heart, he would thereby echo the words of Iblīs: **I am better than him,**[3] and would reap the fruits of the demonic Zaqqūm tree: **He said, "Get down from it! It is not for thee to wax arrogant here. So go forth! Thou art surely among those who are humbled."**[4] The Presence will countenance no arrogance, for it is illuminated by the Light of the Chosen Prophet and his heirs who inherited the station of: "I

1 Q Ṭāhā 20:13.
2 Q Ṭāhā 20:14.
3 Q A'rāf 7:12.
4 Q A'rāf 7:13.

am the master of the children of Adam on the Day of Resurrection, and I do not boast." Nor will it tolerate claims of identity from the one in whom there remains a remnant of his lower self, his passions, and the darkness of his sensorial existence. Thus, the disciple remains in a state of bewilderment, not knowing which of the pronouns to use in order to complete his journey. He is overtaken by bewilderment and sadness, because no matter which of them he mounts, he recognizes an element of pretension and discourtesy. So what is he to do? How can he move between the hammer and the anvil?

Mount the pronoun of "We"—yes, the pronoun of "We." The royal pronoun will stop you at the borders of courtesy between concealing and divulging. For "I" is the pronoun of divulging, and "He" is the pronoun of concealing. With this pronoun, "We," if you are among the possessors of insight, all of your deeds will become blessed and accepted, and your shortcomings will be overlooked. But before that, root your heart in reverence towards the covenant and the pledge of allegiance, and know with certainty that **Truly those who pledge allegiance unto thee pledge allegiance only unto God. The Hand of God is over their hands.**[1] The royal pronoun is the ship of salvation in the ocean of the Lām of Gnosis for the one upon whom the winds of divine success blow, and who rows with the oars of annihilation and reverence towards the secret of the secret.

1 Q Fatḥ 48:10.

Speak through it, worship through it, and exist by it in all your affairs, for it is the celestial steed that will carry you swiftly to the holy center. This is a secret that is only perfected by the astute and insightful disciple.

For the pronoun in the world of letters points to absence and presence. It is divided into separation (*ittiṣāl*) and union (*infiṣāl*). The pronoun "We" is a pronoun of elevation and exaltedness, a pronoun through which the disciple's rank is raised by virtue of the status of his Shaykh. The secret of proximity of the pronoun "We" or *naḥnu* in separation is revealed by the fact that it is written orthographically as *naḥnu*, whereas in union it is orthographically connected to the word, and is represented as *nā* at the end of the word. As such, the disciple's words will be accepted in hearts, and he will be granted support and victory in the physical as well as the spiritual realm through the awe and secrets that are contained within this pronoun.

Verily I perceive a fire

Hast thou heard tell of Moses, when he saw a fire and said unto his family, "Stay here. Verily I perceive a fire. Perhaps I shall bring you a brand therefrom, or find guidance at the fire"?[1]

The eye perceives fire, and the heart perceives Light. The eye perceives something burning, and the heart perceives truth. The sincere disciple is the one who conceals the esoteric realities and does not divulge them. The Lām of Gnosis is the door to entering into the world of realization, and that is where it becomes clear what you are made of, and whether you are worthy of realization or not.

You must accustom your heart to the perspective that every ugly thing is from yourself, while every beautiful thing is from the intermediary. Be like God's Intimate Friend, who attributed harm to himself and all good to the divine Presence when he said, as God tells us: **[The Lord of the Worlds is he] Who created me, and guides me, and Who feeds me and gives me drink, and Who, when I am ill, heals me.**[2] He ascribed illness to himself, even though it issues from God's measuring and decree, out of courtesy towards the presence of the Real. Like-

1 Q Ṭāhā 20:9-10.
2 Q Shuʿarāʾ 26:79-80.

wise, consider how Moses' young servant said: **and naught made me neglect to mention it, save Satan.**[1] Consider too how the Jinn said: **We do not know whether evil is desired for those upon the earth, or whether their Lord desires guidance for them.**[2] They spoke of evil in the passive voice, but ascribed good to God directly. Moreover, a sound hadith reads: "Evil is not from You."[3]

So be the fire that points to the Tree, whose luminous qualities disclose themselves through your fiery deeds, so that those who love burning are attracted to you out of love for the Lord. Thereupon, you will become someone who points to the Presence, and you will have a share alongside every lover of God. The Beloved ﷺ told the door of the city of knowledge, our master ʿAlī, may God ennoble his face: "For God to guide one man by your means would be better for you than to own a wealth of fine red camels."[4] And who is more worthy of going forth to call others than the one whose inner vision God has illuminated? However, let your calling be through your spiritual state before your speech. From the Glass Container (*zujāja*) of your speech, the speaking Lamp discloses itself. God says: **Say, "This is my way. I call unto God with an inner vision—I, and those who follow me. Glory be to God! And I am not among those who ascribe partners unto God."**[5]

1 Q Kahf 18:63.
2 Q Jinn 72:10.
3 Nasāʾī, *Sunan*, K. al-Iftitāḥ, #897.
4 Nawawī, *Riyāḍ al-ṣāliḥīn*, K. al-ʿIlm, #1379.
5 Q Yūsuf 12:108.

You call unto the way of your Lord with an inner vision of certitude; you call unto the firmest handhold while clinging onto it. The station of the Lām of Gnosis is the station of calling to God. It is the station of inviting and making the presence known. You are the one who manifests the Presence within your realm. Thus, the more you master immersion in the Beloved, the more you demonstrate upright adherence to the Law of the Chosen One, and are warmly accepted among creatures on earth and in heaven.

The blessed Messenger of God said, "Abū Dharr, Gabriel sends you his greetings. Abū Dharr, I asked Gabriel the following question, 'Do you know Abū Dharr, Gabriel?' Gabriel said to me, 'How could I not know Abū Dharr, when all the angels in the heavens know him?' I said, 'And how do the angels of the heaven know him?' He replied, 'They know him because of how often he recites *Qul huwa Allāh Aḥad* [Say, He, God, is One].'"[1]

The inhabitants of heaven and earth knew Abū Dharr by of virtue of his annihilation in love for the Messenger of God, through which he inhaled the blessings of Sūrat al-Ikhlāṣ till it became a secret between him and the Messenger of God ﷺ. In this manner, the disciple invokes until a certain act of worship reveals itself to him, and becomes his celestial steed to reach the center of the Presence. These are what we call the Steed-Verses (*āyāt al-rakā'ib*).

1 See al-Rāzī's commentary on Sūrat al-Ikhlāṣ in *al-Tafsīr al-kabīr*.

From Where and to Where?

Rābiʿa, may God be pleased with her, was once asked: "From where, and to where, Rābiʿa?" She replied, "To God we belong, and to Him we return."[1]

Know, dear wayfarer, that journeying to God is not like journeying by God. Journeying to God is for the wayfarers who have not yet reached the Alif of divine unity and the Everlasting Presence, have not pierced through the seventy veils, and have not passed beyond the Lote Tree. As for journeying by God, it is the station of the perfected ones who have completed the readings of the Name, may God be pleased with them.

Know, moreover, that every journey has a point of departure and a point of arrival. At this station, you are journeying from the Hāʾ of Identity to the Lām of Gnosis. You are journeying from yourself, to yourself. We call this the knowledge of the spiritual path (*ʿilm al-ṭarīq*). As for journeying from separation to the secret of messengerhood, that is the science of realization (*ʿilm al-taḥqīq*).

When Rābiʿa replied, may God be pleased with her, she did not say "From the servant to God," or "from this station to that station," which is how a renunciant or a worshipper might have

1 Q Baqara 2:156.

answered. Rather she gave the response of a knower of God; for if she were not one, then she would not have been inspired with that response. This is because the true knower of God never leaves the Name, by which I mean the divine Name Allāh. All of his knowledge is drawn from it and gushes forth from it. As such, he is always swimming in the ocean of **Read by the Name of thy Lord who created.**[1] By the Name of his Lord, which is the divine Name, he reads the true nature of his soul. God manifested to us the Name from the unseen of the unseen, and through it He unites opposites, and through it the loved ones ascend, because the Name does not separate from the Named. Therefore, God's Folk spend their lives, fill their time, and adorn their breaths with the invocation of the divine Name, till they pass away in the invocation and none remains but the Invoked. They continue their luminous ascension until they return to the source of the Name, and through the Names that issue from it, they attain realization of it and adorn themselves with it. For all the Names issue from the divine Name and return to it. They thereby recognize the fountainhead of each Name, along with its specific characteristics, cycle, and esoteric realities. All of this is by direct witnessing through the Kāf of Spiritual Excellence, which is the Light of the perfected heirs of the Prophetic Household, may God be pleased with them all.

Thus, dear wayfarer, the servant does not become "for God," *li'Lāh*, until he passes away in the Lām of Gnosis, and his

1 Q ʿAlaq 96:1.

actions pass away in the actions of the intermediary, so that he sees that all good comes from him from pre-eternity, and that were it not for him, he would not have uttered the primal **Yea**[1] to echo throughout all eternity. If you learn to ascribe all good things back to their rightful owners, all of your possessions become purified, and all things come under your command and fulfill your desires. Even inanimate objects like rocks and trees long for you and seek your spiritual grace. But if you see yourself as possessing spiritual grace, and that the good gushes forth from you and returns to you, while denying the intermediary even in your thoughts, then may God help you.

So learn to anchor your heart to be for God in all your deeds, without seeing yourself as existent, and pass away in love for your shaykh. Let him be your unseen aspect, while you are his visible aspect. He is your spirit and you are his body; he is your heart and you are his container; he is your root and you are his shadow; he is your goal and you are his seeker. In this manner, you shall pass away in him until you start seeing through his vision, and hearing through his hearing, and all of your faculties come from him and to you. Only then will you understand what Abū Bakr, may God be pleased with him, meant when he said, "The blessed Messenger of God ﷺ drank until I was quenched."

1 **And when thy Lord took from the Children of Adam, from their loins, their seeds and made them bear witness concerning themselves, "Am I not your Lord?" they said, "Yea, we bear witness"— lest you should say on the Day of Resurrection, "Truly of this we were heedless."** (Q Aʿrāf 7:172).

The love of the Shaykh is the path of union, and his essence is the gate of entry. He is both gate and gatekeeper, so how do you hope to enter while you still love yourself instead of him, and are engrossed with yourself?

'Abd Allāh b. Hishām related that the Prophet ﷺ was once holding the hand of 'Umar b. al-Khaṭṭāb when 'Umar said: "Messenger of God, you are more beloved unto me than everything except my own soul." The Prophet ﷺ said, "Nay, by the One in Whose Hand is my soul, not until I am more beloved to you than yourself." 'Umar said, "Now, by God, you are indeed more beloved unto me than myself." The Prophet ﷺ said, "At last, 'Umar!"[1]

So do you love your Shaykh more than yourself? Do not respond in word but in deed. God says: **Work, O family of David, in thankfulness, though few of My servants are thankful.**[2]

1 Bukhārī, *Ṣaḥīḥ*, K. al-Aymān wa'l-Nudhūr, #6257.
2 Q Saba' 34:13.

But God threw

God says: **You did not slay them, but God slew them, and you did not throw when you threw, but God threw.**[1]

It is reported that when the army of Quraysh appeared across the valley, the Prophet ﷺ said, "Here come Quraysh with their pride and their pomp! Dear God, I ask You to keep Your promise!" Then Gabriel came to him and said, "Take a handful of dust and throw it at them." When the battle commenced, he said to ʿAlī, "Give me a handful of pebbles from the valley." Then he threw them into the faces of the enemy, crying, "Cursed be your faces!" Every one of them clasped his hands to his eyes, and then they turned and fled, and the faithful routed them, striking them down and taking them prisoner.

God called the Day of Badr the **Day of the Criterion** (*yawm al-furqān*).[2] This alludes to the disclosure-site of separation, for it is the day of annihilation in the acts. On the day when the two sides went to battle, one side did not believe, and so concealed the truth and ascribed the act to themselves, while the other side became annihilated in the blessed Light of the Chosen Prophet, and knew that everything is from God, and that they

1 Q Anfāl 8:17.
2 Q Furqān 8:41.

possessed the form of the act not the act itself, and that while there may be multiple appearances, their reality is God's everlasting secret. Appearances are many: the knife slays, the serpent slays, poison slays, but these are mere appearances whose reality is the flow of the Qur'ān's gathered basmala through the differentiation of the Criterion. Thus the verse reveals this noble truth: **You did not slay them, but God slew them**; for the believers of Badr were worthy of the disclosure of annihilation in the act. The act was therefore ascribed to Him, not them. For the believers, Badr was the manifestation of the differentiating Criterion, making plain the reality of the Qur'ān's all-embracing basmala; and for the Messenger of God ﷺ, it was the reality of annihilation in the Essence and attributes.

So behold, dear wayfarer, how the station of annihilation in the acts caused the believers to be completely forgiven; for it is related that the Messenger of God ﷺ said, "For all you know, it may be that God looked upon the men of Badr and said, 'Do as you please, for I have forgiven you.'"[1]

In this way, dear wayfarer, the more you realize your attribute, the more He assists you with His attribute in the Lām of Gnosis, and your acts pass away in the acts of the Shaykh, so that you see in yourself nothing other than His righteousness and God-consciousness, his night vigils and constant remembrance, his ceaseless prayer. Moreover, it is in the measure of your annihilation and love that you draw replenishment from

1 Bukhārī, *Ṣaḥīḥ*, K. al-Jihād wa'l-sayr, #3081.

him, till you are completely annihilated, and the thrower is your Shaykh, just as the Beloved's ﷺ thrower was God.

As you continue to become annihilated in the acts, you will see the signs of that annihilation. These signs include feeling ashamed to ask for Paradise from God, for how could you ask for Paradise when it seems to you that you have never done anything good in your life? Thus, you will cease to depend upon your deeds, and there will be nothing left to depend upon but God's pre-eternal mercy. **Say, "In the Bounty of God and His Mercy— in that let them rejoice! It is better than that which they amass."**[1]

1 Q Yūnus 10:58.

Then We brought him into being as another creation

God says: **Then We brought him into being as another creation. Blessed is God, the best of creators!**[1]

Know, dear wayfarer, that knowledge of the self—may God grant it to you—is the highest level of knowledge, for to know one's self is even more challenging than to know one's Lord. God says with regard to the Prophet John: **Peace be upon him the day he was born, and the day he dies, and the day he is raised alive,**[2] and with regard to the Messiah he says: **Peace be upon me the day I was born, the day I die, and the day I am raised alive!**[3] With this, God gives us a similitude of the knower of his Lord, upon whom God sends greetings of peace, versus the knower of his own self, who sends greetings of peace upon himself through himself. That is why God praises His Prophet ﷺ at the station of coming close by saying: **The gaze swerved not, nor did it transgress.**[4] For the gaze of the Beloved ﷺ did not swerve from himself, nor did he transgress his true nature by even **two bow's length.** Rather, everything

1 Q Mu'minūn 23:14.
2 Q Maryam 19:15.
3 Q Maryam 19:33.
4 Q Najm 53:17.

was from him and to him. And how could he come out of his noble self, when there is nothing else there but him?

As such, if you wish to plunge into the science of yourself, then return from your lowliness to your elevation, from your human nature to your divine nature. Return from the **lowest of the low** to **the most beautiful configuration**, so that you may understand that you are created upon His image. Return from the clay to the olive, from your bodily nature to the Light of your Shaykh, so that you may recall the Covenant of the Primal **Yea**, and the station of the World of the Seed: **And when thy Lord took from the Children of Adam, from their loins, their seeds and made them bear witness concerning themselves, "Am I not your Lord?" they said, "Yea, we bear witness"— lest you should say on the Day of Resurrection, "Truly of this we were heedless."**[1] You are now in the world of shadows, denying the covenant of the spirits because you are covered in too much clay, and seized by darkness in your states, so that you consider it to be far-fetched to recognize and honor your first Covenant.

For it is in proportion to the amount of clay that is within the creature that there exists, in opposition to it, belief in the unseen and faith. One cannot hope for much success on the spiritual path for the one who is all clay and earth. As for the one who still has some olive in him, you find that he easily acquiesces, surrenders, and affirms the truth, in proportion to how much olive is left in him. Through it, he knows that he lived an

1 Q Aʿrāf 7:172.

immeasurably long life in the loins of his forebears, and dwelled in the seed and the atom until he appeared in the world of shadows. The Chosen One ﷺ said: "The lifespans of the members of my Community are between sixty and seventy, and few of them surpass that age."[1] That is, few members of my Community realize that they have not lived only sixty or seventy years, but have existed since the world of the seed.

So in order to be **brought into being as a new creation** upon the attribute of your Shaykh, you must be constantly faithful to the Covenant of the Primal Yea in all your states. Do not say "there is surrender in my heart, and I love the Shaykh." Love is to pass away in your beloved, and the burden of proof falls upon the claimant. To this effect, I wrote the following poem:

Pour me a cup of love,
and rise above the house of Laylā;

Abrogate the verse of my trace
with the Sūra of the heart;

Serve me the wine of my passion,
and pour the nectar of union;

Enter my city of ecstasy,
where your knowledge will become ignorance;

1 Tirmidhī, *Jāmi'*, K. al-Da'awāt 'an rasūl Allāh, #3550.

Circumambulate me sevenfold,
prostrate and remove your sandals.

O driver of the caravan of hearts,
go gently to the sleepless land.

Do you think love is a discourse,
spoken on the tongue? No!

Love fills the eye with tears,
love strips away the intellect,

Love banishes sleep,
love obliterates images,

Love is the form of the all,
love has no likeness,

Love is the Qibla of Qiblas,
love has a secret sublime.

The Ḥāʾ of Ḥubb (love) carries
the mighty throne of my heart;

The Bāʾ is the dot of my passion,
the ink of my supreme pen.

O dear lovers of my heart,
play the tune of the dead

For a people who died and were
revived by the glorious station of witness.

IV – Separation (*faṣl*)

Nothing is as His like.

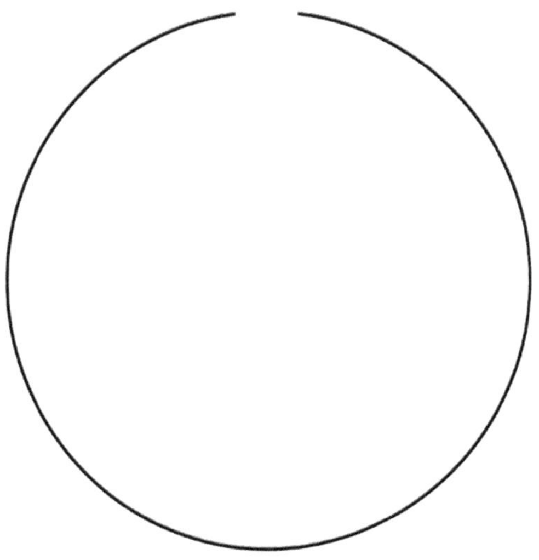

The Cloud (*al-ʿAmāʾ*)

Now, we are about to delve into a tremendous secret which has ever dazzled minds, caused feet to slip, and bested efforts to depict or express it; for there are no determined descents above it, nor imaginalized forms below it. In it, the notion of union vanishes from the disciple's view, and **he can hardly speak clearly**[1] about existence or existent things. This, so that the coin of his spirit may be shaped and polished before it is stamped with the seal of eternal union; for until it has a seal, a coin is not worth anything.

Know, dear passionate disciple, that the site of union in the written form of the divine Name Allāh (الله) is the empty space between the Lām of Gnosis and the Alif of Divine Unity. This is because the word *amāʾ* is formed from four letters. Thus, Separation (*al-faṣl*) is the fourth secret after the Hāʾ of Identity, the Lām of Passionate Love, and the Lām of Gnosis. The disclosure-site of the empty space is manifest, then, but it comprises the origin of all the names, though they **hardly speak clearly**. You will find yourself within it like a boat without a rudder floating upon an ocean without an anchor. All things will come to have a meaning for you inasmuch as things are meaningless.

1 Q Zukhruf 43:52.

What, then, is the Cloud?

Lexically speaking, *amā'* means a fine cloud. This was the answer that the Master of Existence gave to his eminent Companion Abū Razīn when he asked him where our Lord was before He created the heavens and earth; that is, before the manifestation of "where", meaning the six directions, which correspond to the six days in which the heavens and earth were created. He was asking, as it were, about the where before where, the locus of Nowhere.

Know that the Cloud is the wellspring from which burst forth the names of the Real from the level of the Name of the Lord. It is the Nowhere, but from the perspective of the study of the Names in their realm of nonqualification, one could say that it is the first Where. It is sheer essence without relation, because there is no air above it or below it. It is the liminal reality that has receptivity for the differentiation of all nondifferentiated realities, and for the manifestation of all possibilities without restriction. It is like the mirror in which the all is reflected, although the reflection is not a true existent. Rather, it is a disconnected illusion that reflects reality. The Cloud is eternal with respect to the meaning of time that descends from the Aeon, but contingent with respect to the essence of the forms.

Know also that the Cloud is not a place or position, nor a locus or level, nor a location or receptacle; but it is receptive of place, position, locus, level, location, and receptacle. Thus the Master of Existence said, "There is no air above it, and no air below it," so as not to confuse the anthropomorphists who attribute above-ness and spatiality to the divine and confuse the elevated, the Exalted, and the Sublime.

The Aeon (*al-dahr*)

The Aeon is duration without extension, and hence without limits. Endlessness and beginninglessness are one and the same, not merely from a certain perspective. It is sheer passionate love, unshackled from the relationship of lover and beloved. If you could observe the Aeon within linear time, you would see it running in every direction as fast as can be, fixed and stable in itself even as it moves. Then you would cease to have any concept of past to look back on, or future to look forward to, but only the sheer dot of your existence.

This dot is the span (*ḥīn*) of which the Almighty says, **Has there come upon man a span of time in which he was a thing unremembered?**[1] The span is not linear time (*zaman*), nor a moment of measured time (*waqt*); it is the disclosure-site of the Aeon, a sheer divine matter. It is the wellspring of the spiritual opening and uncovering of what lies beyond the veils. Within it, all that never was is folded up, and all of existence from top to bottom is collected. It is the servant's portion of Time itself. I said of this:

1 Q Insān 76:1.

Between the spindle and the distaff lies the secret of intimacy,
A "how" without "how" from the science of the hidden;

The thread of extended illusion, which for us is linear time,
While the moment for us is the measure of mortals.

When the span came as you were in the womb,
You were born alive, though before you were dead.

A span of time wherein you are a firebrand,
One of the realities of the Sublime Essence.

Ask not how, for the how is hidden
In the Sacred Valley, the disclosure-site of allusions.

It is a gathering of the otherness that was dispersed,
A folding-up of everything in heaven and earth.

When it comes to you lovingly and you taste its sweetness,
A draught that is incapacity, a vision of impossibilities;

For can the eye gaze upon its own manifestation,
Or can negation and affirmation coexist?

An authentic hadith on the authority of Abū Bakr tells us that the Prophet ﷺ said, "Time (*al-zamān*) took on its circular form on the day God created the heavens and earth: a year of twelve months, four of which are sacred: three successive, being Dhul-Qaʿda, Dhul-Ḥijja, and Muḥarram, and Rajab, the month of Muḍar between Jumādā and Shaʿbān. What month is this?" His Companions replied, "God and His Messenger know best." He was silent until they began to wonder if he would call it by another name. Finally he said, "Isn't it Dhul-Ḥijja?" They replied, "Indeed it is." He said, "What place is this?" They replied, "God and His Messenger know best." He was silent until they began to wonder if he would call it by another name. Finally he said, "Isn't it the city?" They replied, "Indeed it is." He said, "What day is this?" They replied, "God and His Messenger know best." He was silent until they began to wonder if he would call it by another name. Finally he said, "Isn't it the Day of the Sacrifice?" They replied, "Indeed it is." He said, "Then each of your blood, property, and honor is sacred upon you, as sacred as this day, in this city, in this month of yours. You will meet your Lord, and He will ask you about your deeds, so do not fall into unbelief or error after me, striking one another's necks. Let those who are present convey this to those who are absent, for many a man understands what he hears better than the one who conveys it to him does. Now, have I not conveyed the message?"[1]

The part of this hadith we are interested in presently is his words, "Time took on its circular form on the day God created the heavens and earth." Time took on a circular form, with still-

1 Agreed upon by Bukhārī and Muslim. See Nawawī, *Riyāḍ al-ṣāliḥīn*, K. al-Muqaddimāt, #213.

ness bound up with motion, so that we might understand subsistence through annihilation, and comprehend stillness through motion, and know reality through illusion. Thus time is the measure of the result of the motion of reciprocity; it is, as it were, both motion and the absence of motion, since its disclosure-site is stillness. All the possibilities manifested to infinity, and the unqualified expression of this is stillness. Each present moment is the container of what was measured out in pre-eternity, the time before time. The present moment is the servant's share, for it is through it that he understands essential meaning. The moment is the connection between reality and the disclosure-site of its descent. This is why it is said that "the Sufi is the child of the present moment," and the shaykh of the age is called the Master of the Present Moment.

This diagram may help you understand this better:

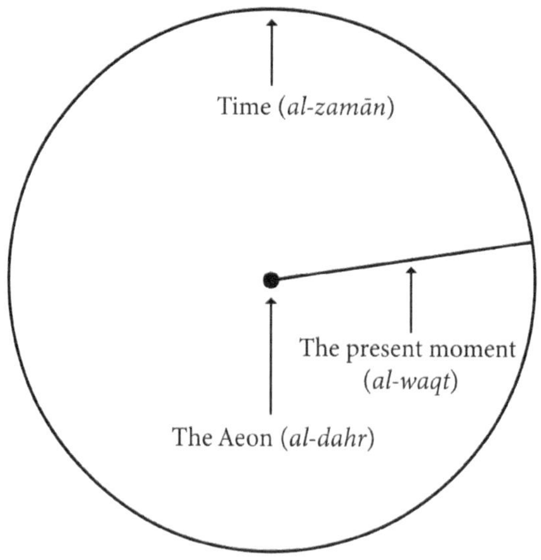

Obliteration (*saḥq*) and Effacement (*maḥq*)

Do you know what obliteration and effacement mean?

The living dead, the silent speaker.

Realizing unletteredness (*ummiyya*) at the loftiest level.

The structure of your being comes to naught, delivering you from the variegation of the veils.

Its riddle is beyond comprehension, for there is no existence.

If obliteration and effacement were to speak, the letters would recoil back into the inkwell.

It is an ocean without water, a wind without a breeze.

It is a drop from the Exclusive Day (*yawm al-aḥad*).

It is that your imprint returns to sand, the footprint of pre-eternity upon you.

It is to perceive the veils in the act of observation (*anẓār*), not in what is observed (*manẓūr*).

It is to see neither good nor evil.

It is to be stripped of your spatial directions.

It is not to be, even as you still know that you are a non-being.

It is for the ocean of the Compeller to stir up and erase the inscription of your name from the sandy shore.

It is for your movements to become the movements of the ocean.

It is to cease to have a shadow.

It is to become the shadow.

It is the point in which the apparent level of the form comes to naught.

It is obliteration and effacement (*ṭams*).

It is to know that the one who speaks is mistaken, while the one who remains silent is in error.

It is an ocean which poses great peril to the one who enters it, yet the one who does not enter will inevitably perish.

It is to find knowledge in ignorance.

The pens are lifted, and the scrolls have dried.

The Isthmus (*al-barzakh*)

God says, **He mixed the two seas, such that they meet one another. Between them lies an isthmus that they transgress not.**[1]

The isthmus is the uniter of the two opposites, the unifier of the two faces; it is not identical with them, nor is it other than them. It is like sleep, the isthmus between life and death. The one who is asleep is neither dead nor alive; he faces both directions without division. Even if the isthmus could be divided, that divided isthmus would require another isthmus, and so on, until we reach the isthmus of isthmuses, which is what we are after.

The isthmus, then, is a level between the world and God, an imaginary line between the shadow and its origin. Likewise, the vegetal world is an isthmus between the animal and mineral worlds, and the soul is an isthmus between the properties of iniquity and reverence: **by the soul and the One Who fashioned it, and inspired it as to what makes it iniquitous or reverent.**[2] It is the level wherein each thing meets its opposite, the venue for the Lord's descent and the servant's ascent, and the

1 Q Raḥmān 55:19-20.
2 Q Shams 91:7-8.

site of the impossible which the delimited intellect cannot grasp. It is also where delimitation occurs, for without the isthmus there would be no distinction between eternity and pre-eternity, manifest and hidden, first and last.

The isthmus is thus a presence of meaning that sits midway between meanings, not a physical place. It can be known, but not perceived. Those who master this science also refer to it as "the where of nowhere" (*ḥaythu lā ḥayth*), for it is the site of the interaction between necessity and negation. It is in this station that we may understand the Holy Saying narrated by Abū Hurayra, may God be pleased with him, in which the Messenger of God ﷺ tells us that God Almighty will say on the Day of Resurrection:

"'O child of Adam, I was sick but you did not visit Me.' He will say, 'Lord, how could I visit you when you are the Lord of the worlds?' He will reply, 'Did you not know that my servant so-and-so was sick, but you did not visit him? Did you not know that had you visited him, you would have found Me with him? O child of Adam, I asked you for food, but you did not feed Me.' He will say, 'Lord, how could I feed You when You are the Lord of the worlds?' God will respond, 'Did you not know that My servant so-and-so asked you for food, but you did not give it to him? Did you not know that had you fed him, you would have found that with Me? O child of Adam, I asked you for water, but you did not give me water.' He will say, 'Lord, how could I give You water when You are the Lord of the worlds?' He will say, 'My servant so-and-so asked you for water, but you did not give it to him. Had you given him water, you would have found that with Me.'"[1]

In this presence, God is receptive of impossible attributes and says, "I was hungry, I was sick, I was thirsty." The servant too is described in impossible ways in this presence, for his attributes are replaced with those of, "I become his hearing with which he hears, his sight with which he sees, his hand with which he strikes, and his foot with which he walks."

The presence of the isthmus can be called the meeting-place of utterances (*majmaʿ al-kalim*) beyond the concept of linear time and delimitation. It is the disclosure-site of the ink of love from which manifest letters, words, and utterances. The Master of the Age emerges from this disclosure-site, propounding the knowledge of all the worlds with a single utterance that comprises all the meanings and words that have ever been and will ever be. It is from this utterance that the voices of all those who invite to the Path can be heard and understood in all their languages—every word, moan, and sigh, the contents of every conscience, the desires of every heart.

The isthmus, then, is a mirror that brings together the attributes and properties of eternity with the qualities and descents of ephemerality. It is the beam between the scales of necessity and possibility. If not for the isthmus, there would be neither angelic transmission nor divine replenishment. Reflect on this.

1 Muslim, *Ṣaḥīḥ*, K. al-Birr wa'l-Ṣila, #4667.

Because of this, the isthmus is the root of existents and the disclosure-site of existence. The balance is maintained through it, because it is identical to the scales themselves. What manifests in it is hidden, and what is hidden in it is manifest; the first in it is last, and the last first; beauty in it is majesty, and majesty beauty; and so on for all the infinite opposites.

The Mantle of Majesty
(*ridā' al-'izza*)

Abū Hurayra related that the blessed Prophet ﷺ told of how God Almighty says, "Pride is My mantle, and magnificence is My lower garment. Should anyone seek to wrest either of them from me, I shall cast him into Hell."[1]

The mantle (*ridā'*) is the garment that covers the top of the body, while the lower garment (*izār*, wrapped around the waist) covers the lower part. The top symbolizes lordship, the lower part servanthood. I have cited this sacred hadith in this chapter in order to evoke the station of lordship, which is covered by the Mantle of Majesty.

Know, dear disciple, that everything has a manifest aspect and a hidden aspect, an outside and an inside. The mantle has two faces, one towards Lordship and the other towards the Cloud. In his ascent when Iblīs came near to the hem of the veil of majesty, he beheld the outside of the mantle. The outside of the mantle is a mirror that reflects the reality of the inner "I" in every soul, for the Names are on the side of the mantle facing lordship. The proof that he drew near to the veil of majesty is that he swore by it when he said, **"Then, by Thy Majesty, I shall**

1 Ibn Ḥibbān, *Ṣaḥīḥ*, K. al-Birr 332.

cause them to err all together, save Thy sincere servants among them."[1] Thus, when his ego was reflected in the mirror of the mantle, he could not bear anything else but for God to envelop him in the protecting embrace of His majesty, so that he would be majestic through God and not merely through his own estimation. However, he supposed that his ascension—which is the nature of the smoke that rises from fire—made him superior to clay, which remains still upon the earth. Thus, he said, "**I am better than him. Thou hast created me from fire, while Thou hast created him from clay.**"[2] And since he believed in his own ascendancy because of his smoky nature, he supposed that Adam's fall to earth disqualified him from the knowledge of the Names. What he did not know was that the greatest Names, those hidden for the disclosures of truth, are apprehended in the realm of servanthood through the Kāf of Spiritual Excellence, upon the surface of this earth.

Beware then, dear wayfarer, of believing in your "I" and imagining that you are better than the Adam of your age, and rejecting the prostration of the pledge of allegiance. Beware of looking down upon the earthly nature of your Mediator when you see him eating food and walking in the marketplace, forgetting that the hereafter is better than the herebelow, and that this manifestation-site is the most ascendant meaning. The remnants of the base soul will remain within you until you take firm hold of your heart as ʿUmar al-Fārūq did when he said,

1 Q Ṣād 38:82-83.
2 Q Aʿrāf 7:12.

"You are more beloved unto me than myself." The sails of the ship of your soul are targets for the arrows of majesty, so halt at the shore of this ocean, may God have mercy upon you, without your ego. Whatever you do, beware of attempting to traverse it, even with your mind, unless you have permission; for this will only end in ruin and disaster. Do not go in unless you hold in your hand the shield of love to protect you from the arrows of majesty.

I composed the following lines about this station:

O driver of the caravan of hearts,
go gently to the sleepless land.

Do you think love is a discourse,
spoken on the tongue? No!

Love fills the eye with tears,
love strips away the intellect,

Love banishes sleep,
love obliterates images,

Love is the form of the all,
love has no likeness,

Love is the Qibla of Qiblas,
love has a secret sublime.

The Ḥāʾ of Ḥubb carries
the mighty throne of my heart;

The Bāʾ is the dot of my passion,
the ink of my supreme pen.

Dear lovers of my heart,
play the tune of the dead

For a people who died and were
revived by the glorious station of witness.

The Stream of Saul

And when Saul set out with the hosts he said, 'Truly God will try you with a stream. Whosoever drinks from it is not of me, and whosoever tastes not of it is of me—save one who scoops out a handful.' But they drank from it, save a few among them. So when he crossed it, he and those who believed with him, they said, 'We have no power today against Goliath and his hosts.' Those who deemed they would meet their Lord said, 'How many a small company have overcome a large company by God's Leave! And God is with the patient.'[1]

Drink it, but do not taste it.

If you are thirsty, beware of drinking.

If you are not thirsty, drink the entire river.

If you scoop out a handful, you will know that you are you, and He is He.

One hand for scooping (*ightirāf*), another for acknowledging (*i'tirāf*).

Not all who cross will be victorious.

You may overcome and win victory, but that is not proof of His approval.

1 Q Baqara 2:249.

Tribulation smelts your ore into pure gold, so that no dross remains in you; but you were gold to begin with, and gold you remain.

You might draw near but be veiled, and you might go far but see Him clearly. You might go far and be veiled, and you might draw near and see Him clearly. Nearness and farness are you, and He is He.

If an Alif appears out of concealment, and the river (*nahr*) becomes daylight (*nahār*), then plunge in, whether secretly or openly.

Sit inside the needle's eye, that you may witness the thread of union in separation.

The difference between Saul (*Ṭālūt*) and Goliath (*Jālūt*) is the difference between Ṭā' and Jīm, but they are all letters.

Iblīs

Know, dear disciple, that Iblīs is one of the manifestations of separation, viewed through the glass of the disclosure-site of the attributes of distance. Yet do not suppose that he is disconnected from you. As long as you are in this station, you must learn how to bring together, not separate. And since he flows through you like blood, he is a part of you, and can reach every part of your being.

Know also that this disclosure-site is the most rebellious manifestation of separation, for he is the prime mover of the soul in its descent to the **lowest of the low**. The one who follows him further and further until the fabric of his being becomes idolatrous darkness will reap nothing but realization of the satanic nature and its properties. This is the reason for the prophetic injunction to make Iblīs' path narrow by blocking it with fasting and hunger.

Farness, then, is the locus of darkness within you, which you call Satan; for closeness to God is not a matter of spatial distance, but rather is a trace from the One who leaves traces, an object of knowledge from the Knower. Beings are far from Him because of the lack of affinity, which is why darkness is the manifestation of farness, and Light is one of nearness. The Almighty says about those who are far from Him: **Upon them is a circle of evil.**[1] The locus of the "circle of evil" (*dāʾirat al-sawʾ*) is farness. The people of Light, on the contrary, are in the locus of nearness according to the levels of the Niche, the Lamp, the Glass, and the Resplendent Planet. The felicitous are only felicitous because of their nearness; the wretched are only wretched because of their farness.

Furthermore, Iblīs can manifest in twelve ways which corresponds to the twelve letters of the testimony of divine unity, *lā ilāha illā Allāh*, but he does not have the power to manifest in the letters of *Muḥammad rasūl Allāh*, because he cannot take on the Prophet's likeness, as stated in the noble hadith: "Whoever sees me in a dream has seen me, for Satan cannot assume my image." Another narration reads, "Whoever sees me in a dream has seen me, for Satan cannot resemble me." Another still has, "Satan may not assume my form." Another has, "Whoever sees me has seen the truth." So Iblīs cannot take on the Prophet's ﷺ likeness, for he is sheer Light. The Prophet ﷺ had no shadow, for Light does not cast a shadow. He was **a shining lamp**,[2] and could see behind him as well as in front of him, for Light has no direction. He could see as well during the night as he could during the day, for he was Light. This is why all darkness is attributed to Iblīs who, as we said,

1 Q Fatḥ 48:6.
2 Q Aḥzāb 33:46.

is the disclosure-site of farness and nonexistence. As for Lights, they are manifestations of nearness, life, and existence.

Know also, dear wayfarer, that the stages of Iblīs' whispered insinuations in this vast ocean begin with the insinuation of separating divine Command from divine Will. For once he has separated them for you, you will either cling to Will and slip, or cling to Command and go astray. Either way, you will suppose that you are virtuous: **Say, "Shall I inform you who are the greatest losers in respect to their deeds? Those whose efforts go astray in the life of this world, while they reckon that they are virtuous in their works."**[1] They reckon they are acting virtuously, but in fact they are following the path of deception and error. **And most of them believe not in God, save that they ascribe partners unto Him.**[2] The one who clings to Will ascribes everything to God, but not in the sense of, **Say, "All is from God"**,[3] for that is the station of annihilation in the divine acts. Instead, he considers that his actions are governed by divine compulsion, and thus follows the example of Iblīs, who said, **Thou hast caused me to err.**[4] With these words he disavows all the commandments and prohibitions in the Book of God, and renders the missions of the prophets and messengers completely pointless, and denies God's proof over His servants.

1 Q Kahf 18:103-104.
2 Q Yūsuf 12:106.
3 Q Nisā' 4:78.
4 Q A'rāf 7:16.

Conversely, the one who clings to Command attributes all his actions to himself and absolves God from them altogether, for of course he knows that God did not create evil! He imagines that this is what he is supposed to believe, but thereby attributes incapacity to God, and makes his own will stronger than the will of the Almighty, who says: **God created you and all that you do.**[1]

Now, if Iblīs successfully prompts you to separate Command from Will, he will plunge you into confusion about free will and predestination, and you will not know whether you are free or compelled. He will not show you all the circles of existence, such that you could attain clarity, but instead he will concentrate your mind on the supreme circle, though you are no match for it and have no knowledge of it. He will goad you into thinking the worst of God, and sow the seeds of doubt in your heart, and water them with what he knows about your past. He will remind you of memories that still move you to anger, and thoughts of just what you would have done if only you had the power to change destiny. He will keep on at you in this way until your heart imbibes this attitude, and it becomes second nature to you.

Then he will begin to delude you with esoteric realities, and illustrate to you how they contravene the divine laws. He will reveal that the Sacred Law is but an illusion, and that unearthing esoteric realities takes priority, since after all there is no

1 Q Ṣāffāt 37:96.

reason to hide them. He will encourage you to disparage the pious works of the Prophets and Messengers. Then he will begin to tempt you to sin, until you become convinced that yes, the Sacred Law is but an illusion. He will find it easy to beckon you, for he can read your thoughts and knows how you are attached to your old ways and nostalgic for the past. If you were a womanizer, he will tempt you to adultery; if you were a drinker, he will tempt you to the bottle. One way or another, he will draw you into sin.

Once you have sinned, this is when the most powerful whispering begins. He laid the grounds for it by first separating Command from Will, then confusing you with free will and destiny, so that you suspected fate and disparaged the divine Laws and Messengers. You no longer have a protective enclosure, or even a Glass, to protect the Lamp of sanctity within you—and so he blows out its flame, and you come to doubt in your Mediator. If you continue to play host to Iblīs and let his suspicions take root in your heart, there will no longer be any difference between you and him.

Dear wayfarer, may God keep you in His care, you must be vigilant and maintain both Command and Will in your heart. Make your body the Law, and your heart the Reality. Be as careful as can be not to suppose that the Law is one thing and the Reality another; for that is nothing but Iblīs' bridle, with which he jerks your head and leads you wherever he pleases, and you become his mount. **He said, "Dost Thou see this, which Thou hast honored above me? If Thou dost grant me reprieve till the Day of Resurrection, I shall surely gain mastery over his progeny, all save a few."**[1]

Make the Reality your lamp and the Law your path. Follow the Sunna of the Chosen Prophet ﷺ in the mirror of your Shaykh, who is your Mediator to your Lord. Demolish Satan's whispers with **Say, 'I seek refuge in the Lord of mankind.'**[2] Hold to servanthood, and venerate lordship, and say, **'Our Lord! We have wronged ourselves. If Thou dost not forgive us and have Mercy upon us, we shall surely be among the losers.'**[3]

1 Q Isrāʾ 17:62.
2 Q Nās 114:1.
3 Q Aʿrāf 7:23.

I Seek Refuge in You from You

Dear God, I seek refuge in You from You.

I seek refuge from proofs, arguments, judgments, and rulings.

I seek refuge in You from seeing You while not being present with You.

I seek refuge in You from the mercy of Your attributes.

I seek refuge in You from Light that veils me from You.

I seek refuge in You from the tremble of passionate love that makes me absent from Your passionate love.

I seek refuge in You from being one who seeks (*ṭālib*) or one who flees (*hārib*).

I seek refuge in You from being near or far.

I seek refuge in You from descending and ascending.

I seek refuge in You from speaking the truth.

I seek refuge in You from Paradise.

I seek refuge in You from invocation.

I seek refuge in You from knowledge that serves as proof for You.

I seek refuge in You from resolve that causes my soul to surpass others by its caprice.

I seek refuge in You from knowledge that is transmitted.

I seek refuge in You from falsehood that escapes me, or truth that seizes me.

I seek refuge in You from gnosis that I take as a god.

I seek refuge in You from the sin of gnosis that obliterates my ignorance.

I seek refuge in You from gnosis that causes me to deny You.

I seek refuge in You from the guise of knowledge through which I would worship my caprice.

I seek refuge in You from knowledge of the herebelow and the hereafter.

I seek refuge in You from letters and the shapes that are created therefrom.

I seek refuge in You from every name that crowds my vision.

I seek refuge in You from asking You.

I seek refuge in You from not asking You.

I seek refuge in You from opposition, not from the two opposites.

I seek refuge in You from a lying heart and a truthful tongue.

I seek refuge in You from forgiveness that I seek out of fear, or a supplication that I make out of need.

I seek refuge in You from a gaze wherein I suppose myself to be the gazer, not the gazed upon.

I seek refuge in You from the affliction of asking for an affliction to be lifted.

I seek refuge in You from the specificity of lifting the veils, not the all-inclusiveness of beholding the veil.

I seek refuge in You from unveiling and the veil.

I seek refuge in You from a vision that veils me from seeing You.

I seek refuge in You from a remedy wherein I do not see the illness.

I seek refuge in You from any certainty that does not contain misgivings that direct me to You.

I seek refuge in You from the defiance of seeking Your approval.

I seek refuge in You from witnessing words, not from bearing witness.

I seek refuge in You from a qibla that has a direction, and from all directions.

I seek refuge in You from a prayer that has a beginning and an end.

I seek refuge in You from fasting the month, not the month of fasting.

I seek refuge in You from embarking upon a pilgrimage (*ḥajj*) to a stone (*ḥajar*).

I seek refuge in You from the faith of multiple levels.

I seek refuge in You from the benevolence of divine immanence (*iḥsān al-tashbīh*).

I seek refuge in You from the transcendence of divine benevolence (*tanzīh al-iḥsān*).

I seek refuge in You from my own act of affirming all these things by seeking refuge from them, since they are not You, and You are hallowed beyond all of it.

The Two Bows of Love

Know that I present this chapter to you in the context of the discourse about separation, because there is a certain correlation between separation and nondelimitation, in the sense that separation is the disclosure-site of nondelimitation. The same goes for love, for those who have experienced its burning. For the people of love, love is a transcendent meaning that is not delimited; and the two bows serve merely to illustrate this meaning, not to delimit it. Love is a tremendous transcendent meaning, an attribute of God Himself as well as His servant, just like the name the Friend *al-Walī*. The Almighty says, **Truly God loves those who repent, and He loves those who purify themselves;**[1] **And be virtuous. Truly God loves the virtuous;**[2] **And when thou art resolved, trust in God; truly God loves those who trust;**[3] **They did not then falter in the face of what befell them in the way of God, nor did they weaken, nor did they demean themselves. And God loves the patient.**[4] And in an authentic hadith: "My servant does not draw near to Me with anything more beloved to Me than what I have made

1 Q Baqara 2:222.
2 Q Baqara 2:195.
3 Q Āl ʿImrān 3:159.
4 Q Āl ʿImrān 3:146.

obligatory upon him; and My servant continues to draw near to me with voluntary deeds until I love him. When I love him, I become his hearing with which he hears, his sight with which he sees, his hand with which he strikes, and his foot with which he walks. Were he to ask of Me, I would surely give him, and were he to seek refuge with Me, I would surely grant him refuge."[1]

There is no better station than this for love to be disclosed, purified from the turbidities of the veils. In it there are no veils to distract, nor forms to confuse. This is where love begins and makes its imprint upon the earth of the heart like two bows, which delimit love from the servant and love from the Lord, like this:

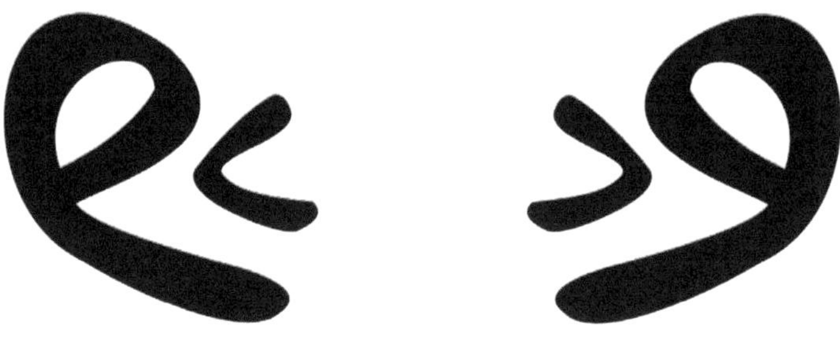

This is therefore the delimitation of an unqualified meaning that cannot truly be delimited, for nothing remains but love. It

1 Bukhārī, *Ṣaḥīḥ*, K. al-Riqāq, #6502.

is a delimitation from itself to itself, as though you are in an ocean but enraptured by a single drop of it, such that there is really no delimitation going on.

The word *ḥubb* حب (love) is composed of two letters, Ḥā' and Bā', which have the numerical value of 8+2, meaning that the total value of the word *ḥubb* is 10.

Likewise, the word *widd* ود (a synonym for *ḥubb*) is composed of the two letters Wāw and Dāl, which have the values 4+6, so its total value is also 10.

In this station the lover is, as it were, so consumed with love that he forgets the Beloved. This is a rarefied state that overcomes the seeker in this station. It is related that Laylā once approached Qays as he was crying out, "Laylā, Laylā!", pressing chunks of ice to his breast which melted instantly from the heat of his heart. Laylā greeted him and said, "Here I am, the object of your desire. I your beloved, the coolness of your eye. I am Laylā!" He turned to her and said, "Be gone! I have no time for you now, I'm busy with my love for you!"

There is another state that may overcome the seeker, such as once visited Ibn 'Arabī, may God sanctify his spirit, as he related in the *Meccan Openings*:

"The faculty of imagination once carried me to the point where my love would summon my beloved before my eyes in bodily form from out of nowhere, in the manner in which Gabriel would appear before the Messenger of God ﷺ. Though I could not bring myself to look at him, he spoke to me and I listened and understood. He left me in such a state that for days

I would eat no food, for every time a meal was served to me he would stand by the table and look at me, and say with a voice I could hear with my own ears, 'Do you really mean to eat, even as you look upon me?' So I would go without eating, but feel no hunger, instead filling myself with him until I had grown fat upon my beholding of him, for the vision took the place of food for me. My friends and family were amazed at how stout I had grown despite not eating, as for many days I went without tasting food or drink, but felt neither hunger nor thirst. Yet the vision never left me for a moment, whether I was standing or sitting, moving or at rest."[1]

In this station, the seeker's state is that he encounters no station, attribute, or form to cling to, but remains floating in the ocean of incorporeal abstractions, which is an ocean without a shore. In this condition, love sheds the Mīm of *al-mawjūd*, the existent, and becomes *al-wujūd*, existence itself. When he attains realization and mastery of this, love becomes his food, drink, and the very air he breathes.

1 Ibn ʿArabī, *Futūḥāt*, II, 325; cf. Corbin, *Creative Imagination*, p. 382.

The Nearness of Passion

How can you love one who has no form? How can you feel passion for one who is beyond compare?

In the midst of the station of passionate love (*'ishq*) and the waves of desire, love mingles with your flesh and blood and becomes your all, and you draw **within two bows' length or nearer** of union. You are at the door of the inner heart's husk. God says of those who cover this reality and become oblivious to it: **That is God, your Lord; to Him belongs sovereignty. As for those upon whom you call apart from Him, they do not possess so much as the husk of a date stone.**[1] The husk (*qiṭmīr*) is the skin on the date stone. When yearning for the divine self-disclosure is great, it sets the wick of imagination in the heart ablaze with the fuel of the Kāf of Conviction—but without any form. Preparedness to breathe in the Alif of Divine Measure (*alif al-taqdīr*) is from His All-Mercifulness, which envelops all existents.

God says, **Thy Lord decrees that you worship none but Him.**[2] Everything that the servant loves, every object of his affection and inclination, is a descent from the names of the Real, veiled with the forms of existents. But this station will not

1 Q Fāṭir 35:13.
2 Q Isrā' 17:23.

brook the manifestation of these forms, for it is the venue of the first manifestation of the Nearness of Passion, which is the beauty that is hidden in every form with which the divine Identity veils itself.

God says, **Say, "If you love God, then follow me, God will love you and forgive you your sins. And God is Forgiving, Merciful."**[1] By **God will love you** [***yuḥbibkum***], He means the reality of His Self, which is why the double-B of *ḥubb* is split into two distinct instances of the Bā' in the verb here, so that you see the Bā' through the Bā', not merely added together in the manner of doubled letters as if the second is a supererogatory compliment of the first, and a reflection of the form, but rather each letter being essential and true to its origin. Its origin, moreover, is the reality of glorification and transcendence. God says: **Glorify the Name of thy Lord, the Most High, Who created, then proportioned; Who measured out, then guided.**[2] All of existence is proportioned according to the Alif of Divine Measure and the measures of guidance, so that you may apprehend how the Presence can be truly transcendent in the forms of existents. The first of its disclosures is the dervishes of the Presence, for they are the nearest disclosure-site of this transcendence because of how near they are to the presence of union.

1 Q Āl 'Imrān 3:31.
2 Q A'lā 87:1-3.

V – Union (*waṣl*)

Glorify the Name of thy Lord, the Most High, Who created, then fashioned; Who measured out, then guided.

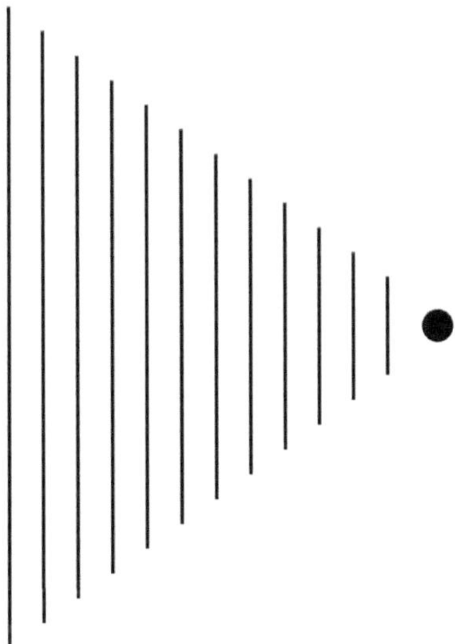

And They Say, "Five"

Know, dear disciple, that most of those who have spoken about esoterism have done so without having any basis in true unveiling or correct knowledge. They merely speculate based on the conjectured forms that they construct in the intellect, and the caprice that takes hold of the lower self. God says, **They follow naught but conjecture and that which their souls desire.**[1] They follow only their limited intellectual conjectures; and since their intellects do not conform to the Supreme Intellect, the intellect of the Chosen Prophet ﷺ, their understanding and knowledge is necessarily subordinate to the principle of caprice. **Then We placed thee upon a clear path from the Command; so follow it, and follow not the caprices of those who know not.**[2] Their intellects cannot grasp what lies beyond the physical eye, and so all that is left is to conform to conjecture and interpret scripture with caprice. A tradition says, "Caprice is the worst idol worshipped on earth." The blight of the minor intellect is its dependence on forms to achieve understanding. When I say "the minor intellect," I mean the physical mind that is nowadays called the brain. They attempt to esoterically interpret unseen things on the basis of things that corre-

1 Q Najm 53:23.
2 Q Jāthiya 45:18.

spond to them by name, then they apply the sensory forms to the unseen. This method yields them nothing but error. Yet when this way of thinking becomes second nature to a person, his soul becomes assured that it is the truth and that all else is false. This is why they worship their caprice, and are the furthest of people from the truth.

Let us return to our present discussion: **And they say, "Five."**[1] That is, those who judge by outward appearances wish to build the temple of Law over the folk of esoteric Truth.[2] Here in the station of union, dear disciple, you must learn how to perfect shutting out the vision of anyone but the People of Light, and being oblivious to all but them. For the ones who have a connection to the Presence, the folk of spiritual poverty and surrender, are the standard of Light. As for all others, they have no existence at all, and your attitude towards them should be limited to showing them the courtesies of the Sacred Law by treating them with kindness and mercy. The Messenger of God ﷺ said, "A Muslim owes his fellow Muslim six things: when you meet him, give him greetings of peace. When he calls you, answer him. When he asks you for advice, advise him. When

1 Q Kahf 18:22.

2 **And in this way We caused them to be discovered, that they might know that God's Promise is true, and that there is no doubt about the Hour. When they were disputing among themselves about their affair, they said, "Erect a building over them; their Lord knows them best." Those who prevailed over their affair said, "We shall build a place of worship over them."** Q Kahf 18:21.

he sneezes and praises God, bless him. When he falls ill, visit him. When he dies, follow his funeral procession."[1]

They say, "[They were] three, and the fourth was their dog." And they say, "Five, and the sixth was their dog"—guessing at the unseen. And they say, "Seven, and the eighth was their dog." Say, "My Lord knows best their number; none know them save a few."[2] The people differed concerning the number of this unprecedented presence, all hoping that they might be among those **few** who knew it. Yet they were certain about the dog and always included it, as if the dog were at the center of the equation; and it was through the dog's secret that the three, the five, and the seven were affirmed.

Now, we are discussing the station of union, the station of the **five**, the station of the primal flow of the Handful. It was the dog who affirmed the **five**, for he was the primal **sixth**, while the **five** were descents, measures, and variegations of his reality. Their length was delimited, unlike his, and their color was known, unlike his. His was the primal union inasmuch as he was the door of arrival for the Alif of Eternity; and his was also the primal separation inasmuch as he was their **fourth**. No one could measure him or represent him, for he was nonexistence.

The **five**, then, symbolize union, and the Sleepers of the Cave are the secrets of the heart, for the heart is the cave of esoteric realities. This union is the manifestation-site of the master of

1 Muslim, *Ṣaḥīḥ*, K. al-Salām, #2162b.

2 Q Kahf 18:22.

the dog, who was nonmanifest in his essence and manifest through his dog. This was due to his deep humility, a humility which is impossible for any but the folk of love and nearness who share his form. To have mastery over existence while walking among people upon the earth as the lowliest of them—that is true humility. Those who have mastery over nothing cannot practice renunciation, for what do they have to renounce?

These, then, are allusions in this station to the disciple, showing him how he must learn to interact with those who have a connection to the Presence, until his heart imbibes the quality of union and its secrets are manifested to him both in the sensory realm and the realm of pure meaning. For when the Shaykh gifts one of the secrets of the presence to the disciple, he makes the entire circumference of his being float in this secret. That is, whether he graces you with the **fifth** secret, or the **third**, or whatever secret it may be, your entire circumference will receive this secret. All you have to do is understand and reflect, so that the treasure that was hidden from you may come to Light.

The Outline of Union

God Almighty says: **Say, "Call upon Allāh, or call upon the All-Merciful. Whichever you call upon, to Him belong the Most Beautiful Names.**[1]

In order for you to perceive the meaning of the Hidden Alif and its secret within the outline of union, you must first learn the meaning of the measuring-out (*taqdīr*), then the measure (*qadr*) of the name the All-Merciful (*al-Raḥmān*), the rank of the *Alif*, and the disclosure-site and shadow of the basmala. I will explain each of them to you one by one, so that you understand the disclosures of union and the movement of the Lights in this station.

The Name of the All-Merciful (*al-Raḥmān*)

Know, may the Lord have mercy upon you and give you success in attaining His approval, that the name the All-Merciful is the totality of the oaths that God swears by in the holy Book: Alif-Lām-Rā', Ḥā-Mīm, Nūn. Moreover, it is the master and the king of the names, because it is the disclosure-site of the Essence along with the divine name Allāh: **Say, "Call upon Allāh, or call upon the All-Merciful."**

1 Q Isrā' 17:110.

God says: **My Mercy embraces all things.**[1] Thus, this name is the flow of existence within every existent, and it is this name that embraces all things. It embraces the multiplicity of the names. It embraces their attributes in respect of the disclosures and Lights. It embraces their traces in the disclosure-site of existents. If it were not for the All-Merciful, then nonexistence would have preponderance over existence in the cosmic composites. It is thus the mercy of necessity that is not absent from any particle, and it flows in the same measure through existents. Thus, the disclosure-site of the mercy of necessity from the name the All-Merciful in Paradise is identical to the one in Hell. If you deny the existence of mercy in Hell, then read the verse: **My Mercy embraces all things**, and remember that Hell is a thing. Read also the verse revealed on the tongue of Abraham the Intimate Friend, may God invoke blessings upon him and upon our Prophet: **O my father! Truly I fear that a punishment from the All-Merciful will befall you, such that you will become a friend of Satan.**[2]

Thus, one aspect of this name's grandeur is that it is paired with the divine name Allāh. Moreover, you should know that even for the invokers of the divine name Allāh, nothing comes out from their inner selves except the name al-Raḥmān—except for the perfected invokers among them. This is why one noble hadith concerning the creation of our master Adam, upon him and our Prophet be blessings and peace, relates that he was cre-

1 Q Aʿrāf 7:156.
2 Q Maryam 19:45.

ated in the image of the name Allāh, while another narration states that he was created in the image of the name al-Raḥmān.

The Measuring (*al-taqdīr*)

The measuring is the manifestation of the most low bearing the secret of the most high, in order for glorification (*tasbīḥ*), which is the declaration of holiness (*taqdīs*) and incomparability (*tanzīh*), to take place. God says: **Glorify the Name of thy Lord, the Most High.**[1] It is the manifestation-site of true existence at the levels of determination. Thus, the measuring out gives the scale for each level in respect of its rightful due and worth according to the standards of perfection and beauty. If you understood the measuring, you would truly experience the disclosure of the verse: **No disproportion dost thou see in the All-Merciful's creation.**[2]

From the perspective of divine power (*qudra*), the measuring is the forms of possible things within the entities, so that the world may become known. From the perspective of the Powerful (*al-Qādir*), the measuring is that through which the knower is known. Thus, the measuring is a manifestation through nonmanifestation; He manifested the measuring in order for the power and the Powerful to become nonmanifest. The measuring is not a descent; rather, the descent becomes manifest through the measuring. For were it not for the measuring, there would be no descents or ascensions. Likewise, the measuring

1 Q Aʿlā 87:1.
2 Q Mulk 67:3.

can be seen in the disclosure of the descent, for were it not for the descent, the measuring would not be grasped. The measuring therefore is the scale of descent, and the descent is the manifestation of the measuring.

The Level of the Alif

Know, may God have mercy on you, that the Alif is not a letter in its essence, for it is the first thing that the dot brought down when it inclined away from the Center through the secret of "I loved to be known." Thus, it is the sultan, and it possesses the divine attribute of self-subsistence. It is called Alif because it brings together (*ta'alluf*) the letters. The latter are its attribute that bear resemblance to it; the Alif is their union, and they are its separation. The Alif is the perfect vicegerent in the world of letters, and it manifests through them. However, **faculties of sight do not perceive**[1] the Alif. The reason people are veiled from seeing the Alif in the disclosure-sites of its flow is that they delimit it in specific forms, so that the blessing of the secret of the Alif in the disclosure-sites of the letters escapes them.

However, the Alif that we are speaking of here is not the Original Alif (*al-alif al-aṣlī*), but the Hidden Alif (*al-alif al-muqaddar*) in the name al-Raḥmān (الرحمٰن) between the Mīm and the Nūn, which is alluded to in the verse: **On the Day when the shank is laid bare and they are called to prostrate, yet are not able.**[2]

1 Q Anʿām 6:103.
2 Q Qalam 68:42.

The Basmala

Know, dear disciple, may God assist you in attaining all that is good, that each letter of B-S-M (*bismi*) is a triangle in the image of the disclosure-site of the worlds. The Bāʾ *comprises Bāʾ, Alif, Hamza*; the Sīn comprises *Sīn, Yāʾ, Nūn*; and the Mīm comprises *Mīm, Yāʾ, Mīm*. This is the tether of the celestial mount at this disclosure-site, because the basmala in the mirror of the spiritual realm (*malakūt*) is a triangle composed of the Bāʾ of *bismi*, the Nūn of *al-Raḥmān*, and the Yāʾ of *al-Raḥīm*. In the disclosure-site of the sensory realm, it casts a shadow when the sun of manifestation shines upon it; and that is the cubical basmala, an upper triangle along with its shadow.

The Bridge of Union Through the Names

God says: **This indeed is My straight Path; so follow it, and follow not the other roads, lest they separate you from His way. This He has enjoined upon you, that haply you may be reverent.**[1]

Know, dear disciple, that we have placed this chapter here in order for you to find correct guidance and a clear understanding of union, if it is decreed for you to taste separation. Thereby you may understand that the Path (*ṣirāṭ*) is disclosure-site of union between the Lām of Gnosis and the Alif of Exclusive Singularity (*tafrīd*) and Spiritual Excellence (*iḥsān*); and that this Path is a terrifying bridge connecting one lover to the other. This bridge is traced by the extent of your union, love, and yearning in the presence of transcendent passionate love, that through it you may come to rest in the eternal abode with the Prophets, Messengers, and righteous servants of God. **What beautiful companions they are!**[2]

Know, God have mercy on you, that since the world is God's words, and since the Chosen One is the comprehensive unifier of all words, he governs over all generations from the first to the last, and therefore is the first of the Prophets and the Seal of the

1 Q An'ām 6:153.
2 Q Nisā' 4:69.

Prophets. The Law that he sets down, therefore, is the disclosure-site of the path of union, by virtue of the countless meanings of the divine names that it carries. The unswerving and tolerant Law (*ḥanīfiyya samḥā'*) is thus the disclosure-site of union that will carry you over Hell in the Hereafter. The breadth of this bridge is commensurate with the outward righteous deeds that you make for your soul in this abode. The swiftness with which you will pass over it is in the measure of your inward deeds and their purity from hooks and thorns, and in measure of the purity of your intention and sincerity, and the reverence (*taʿẓīm*) and surrender (*taslīm*) that you harbor within your deepest self.

The bridge is of two sorts: imminent, and yet to come. The yet to come is well-known, as described in the hadiths. As for the imminent bridge, it is the one which the disciple must struggle and strive to traverse; for "He whose beginning is illuminated, his end is illuminated." This imminent bridge is the one upon which you traverse the stations and phases that lead to the courtyard of God's exclusive singularity (*tafrīd*) and direct witnessing (*shuhūd*), where the truth is realized. It is there that you will realize the disclosure-site of union of the witnesser and the Witnessed. This bridge is raised over the fire of the lower self, and the blazing flames of egoism. Its fire is more intensely vehement than the Fire that God threatens us with, even though the disciple may forget its heat just as a sick person forgets the pain of his illness when he thinks of something that has a stronger hold on his heart. Similarly, the traveling disciple forgets about the heat of the egoic fire because his intellect is deceived by the pleasures of forms and impressions, to the point that he completely forgets his pain, and imagines himself to be healthy, though he is far from that.

Moreover, just as the disciple's fire is more intense than God's threatening Fire, his garden is unlike the Garden of delights. It is the garden of gnostic sciences, which is the Lote Tree of the Furthest Boundary beyond the amorous peers (*ḥūr*) and the palaces (*quṣūr*), where there is only the Lord of the amorous peers and the castles.

The bridge of union is His beautiful names, whose outward sum total is one-hundred minus one. The one "who reckons them"[1] enters the garden of gnostics sciences, let alone the Garden of delights. To this effect, God's Messenger drew a line with his hand and said: "This is God's straight path (*sabīl*)." Then he drew lines to its right and to its left, and he said: "As for these paths, there is a devil upon each of them, inviting to it." It is self-evident that a line is drawn from the furthest point to the closest point. That is, God's Path arrives to the Prophet ﷺ, its route passing through the ascending degrees of the divine names, whose delimitation in the realm of possibility is the Sacred Law, and whose luminous quality is the most sublime secret which is the Muḥammadan Reality.

1 A reference to the hadith: "To God belong ninety-nine names; one-hundred minus one. Whoever reckons them enters the Garden." Bukhārī, *Ṣaḥīḥ*, K. al-Shurūṭ, #2736.

Thus, dear disciple, if you wish to be among the people of union, you must gather the beautiful names within your true self. For the secret of the names lies in their gathered totality. God says: **He taught Adam all the names,**[1] and the totality of the names is the secret of union of the everlasting presence.

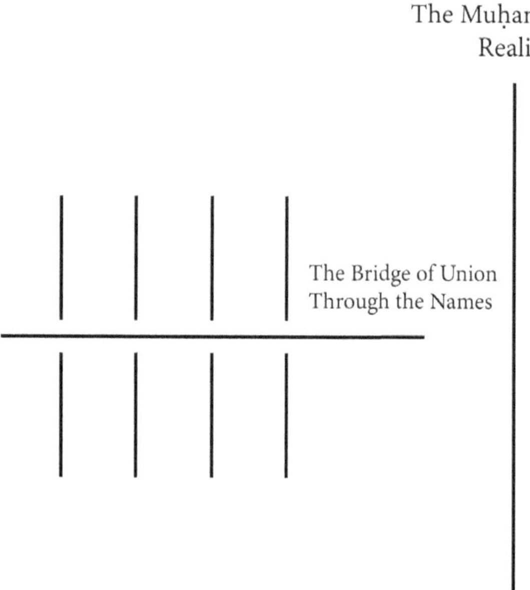

1 Q Baqara 2:31.

The Name of the All-Merciful (*ism al-Raḥmān*)

Know, may the Lord have mercy upon you and give you success in attaining His approval, that[1] God distinguishes in His Book between the servants of Allāh and the servants of the All-Merciful. The servants of Allāh are the great saints, Messengers, and Prophets, as He says in the case of the Chosen Prophet ﷺ: **When the servant of Allāh rises to call upon Him, they well-nigh swarm upon him."**[2] As for the servants of the All-Merciful: **The servants of the All-Merciful are those who walk humbly upon the earth, and when the ignorant address them, say, "Peace."**[3] They walk upon the earth of humility in a tranquil manner by virtue of the luminous attributes and majestic Essence that they witness.

To this effect, one report states, "I saw people from my Community who have not yet been created, and who will come after this day. I love them, and they love me. They extend sincere counsel and generosity to one another. They walk with God's Light gently among people, with discretion and reverence.

1 A repeat from the passage in the chapter, "The Outline of Union" (*Rasm al-Wasl*) is omitted above.

2 Q Jinn 72:19.

3 Q Furqān 25:63.

They are safe from people, and people are safe from them, by virtue of their patience and forbearance. Their hearts echo with the remembrance of God.[1] Their mosques are filled with their prayers. They are merciful to their young,[2] and respectful to their elders. They comfort one another. The wealthy among them look after the poor, and the strong look after the weak. They visit their sick, and attend their funerals." Thereupon a man in the group said, "Are they kind to their slaves?" The Prophet ﷺ turned to him and replied, "No, they do not own slaves. They serve themselves. They are too noble to ask God for luxury, because of how lowly the herebelow is in the eyes of their Lord." Then the Prophet ﷺ recited: **The servants of the All-Merciful are those who walk humbly upon the earth.**

No one knows the reality of this name except for those who assume the characteristics of His name the Aware, *al-Khabīr*: **The All-Merciful: so ask, regarding Him, one who is aware,**[3] namely the perfected gnostics. The perfected shaykh, therefore, is the one who has experiential awareness of the divine presence both in summary and in detailed differentiation, in nondelim-

1 The Shaykh here appears to be quoting from *al-Baḥr al-Madīd* where this is cited as *qulūbuhum bi-dhālika ilayhi yarji'ūn*. In al-Tha'labī's Tafsīr, however, it is cited as *qulūbuhum bi-dhikr Allāh yarji'ūn*, which makes more sense. Ibn 'Ajība's quotation appears to be a misprint or scribal error, as Ibn 'Ajība attributed it to al-Aslamī, from which al-Tha'labī also narrated it with a chain of transmission, so we assume Ibn 'Ajība took it from al-Tha'labī.

2 Likewise, al-Tha'labī has *ṣaghīr*, rather than *ḍa'īf*, which seems more likely given the context.

3 Q Furqān 25:59.

itation and delimitation. Moreover, we only call him a perfected shaykh on account of his understanding of the secret of the divine mounting of the Throne, from and to himself. That is why the Arab unbelievers denied the name al-Raḥmān: **And when it is said unto them, "Prostrate before the All-Merciful," they say, "And what is the All-Merciful? Shall we prostrate before that [to] which you command us?" And it increases them in aversion.**[1] But they did not deny the divine name Allāh, for they claimed of their false gods, **We do not worship them, save to bring us nigh in nearness unto Allāh.**[2] They rejected al-Raḥmān although the world subsists through the flow of this Breath (*nafas*) and the outspreading of mercy that is the Muḥammadan Mīm. For this reason, the open vowel (*fatḥa*) above the Mīm of *al-Raḥmān* alludes to the outspreading of mercy across the worlds. I only mention this to you so that this name takes on great importance in your heart, because it is among the greatest keys to gnosis, and the towering minarets of union.

I have placed this name in this chapter because of the Hidden Alif between the Mīm and the Nūn, about which God says: **On the Day when the shank is laid bare and they are called to prostrate, yet are not able.**[3] An authentic tradition relates that Abū Saʿīd, may God be pleased with him, said, "I heard the holy Prophet ﷺ say, 'Our Lord will lay bare His shank, and every

1 Q Furqān 25:59.
2 Q Zumar 39:3.
3 Q Qalam 68:42.

believing man and woman will prostrate themselves before Him. But there will remain those who used to prostrate in the world in order to be seen and heard. They will attempt to prostrate themselves, but their backs will become [so stiff that it is] as though they had one vertebra.'"[1]

None will prostrate save those whose bodily posture can assume the Lām's curvature of love. Do you not see that the Lām has the ability to become curved? As for the one who is ridden by his ego, and whose "I" is his wont, and who ascribes his lower self as partner with God, and sees himself as existing alongside God's existence, he will have no ability to prostrate, because the Alif does not possess the curvature of the Lām. His prostration thus becomes a fall and a disgrace. We seek refuge in God from being deprived after receiving generosity!

1 Bukhārī, *Ṣaḥīḥ*, K. Tafsīr al-Qur'ān, 4635.

The Nondelimitation of Delimitation and the Delimitation of Nondelimitation (*iṭlāq al-tayqīd wa-taqyīd al-iṭlāq*)

Know, may God have mercy on you, that I placed this chapter here in order for you to know, then to work on, how the flow occurs in the disclosure-site of separation and union. This disclosure-site requires of you that you perfect the delimitation of nondelimitation. For the all-comprehensive name Allāh, which refers to the Essence, is nondelimitation inscribed upon nondelimitation. However, in order for our union with the Holy Presence to take place, it manifests in letters, and discloses itself through the Alif, the two Lāms, and the Hā', and thus becomes delimited by letters. I use these words in a figurative sense, in order to be able to say anything at all, because when delimitation disappears, speech comes to naught, and all that remains is incapacity, bewilderment, and the spiritual state that is produced by them.

Thus, even though the all-comprehensive Name appears delimited by letters, the disclosure-site of nondelimitation in it is between the Lām of Gnosis (*lām al-ʿirfān*) and the Alif of Divine Unity and Demonstrative Knowledge (*alif al-tawḥīd wa'l-burhān*). Moreover, you learn delimitation from the flow through the Hā' and the two Lāms, i.e., the Lām of Passion and the Lām of Gnosis. However, when you arrive at separation, you must become liminal (*barzakhī*) between the high and the low, between the basmala and its shadow, so that you may taste all of the presences.

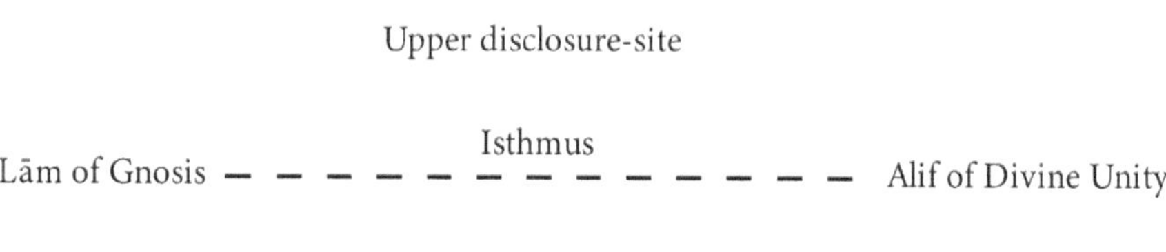

For in the disclosure-site of the Hā' of Identity that we are currently discussing, the Hā' of Identity manifests itself through the circle, which is an expression of delimitation, whose non-delimitation is the Lām of Passionate Love with respect to the second reading that is expressed as *huwa* at this phase. As for the separation and union of the Hā', which are the forth and the fifth readings of the Hā' of Identity, the delimitation of non-delimitation is through *Lillāh*, "to God."

When I say delimitation (*taqyīd*) at this disclosure-site, it is not the delimitation of the human being that discloses itself through the sensory realm. Rather, it is a delimitation of the spirits in the disclosure-site of the spiritual realm (*malakūt*), just as it was for the Virgin Mary when the spirit disclosed itself to her as a **proportioned man.**[1] The pure meaning of the

1 Q Maryam 19:17.

transcendent spirits became delimited for her in the disclosure-site of the spiritual realm, not the physical realm. For only those who master the secret of the cosmic laws (*aṣḥāb sirr al-nawāmīs al-kawniyya*) can bring down that which is transcendent into the visible realm of the senses. This, moreover, is what occurred to the noble Companions with the Chosen Prophet ﷺ. For everyone saw the man dressed in white clothing, which we know because of how ʿUmar al-Fārūq, who narrated the hadith, said, "traces of travel were not visible upon him, and none of us knew him."[1] Then the Chosen Prophet told them that it was Gabriel who had come to teach them their religion.

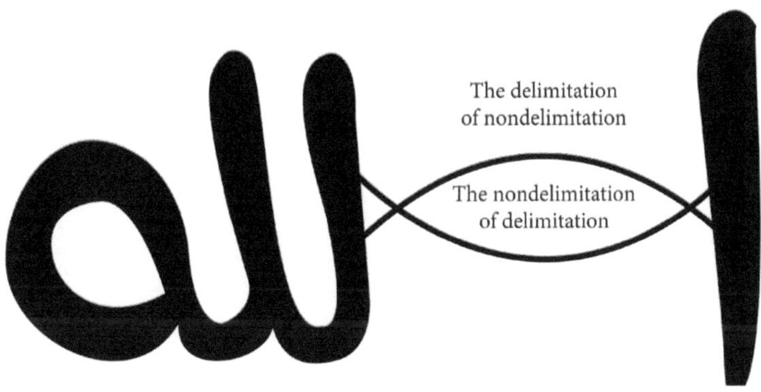

1 Nawawī, *al-Arbaʿūn al-nawawiyya*, #2.

The Measuring (*al-taqdīr*)

God says: **Glorify the Name of thy Lord, the Most High, Who created, then fashioned, Who measured out, then guided.**[1]

The measuring is the manifestation of the most low bearing the secret of the most high, in order for glorification (*tasbīḥ*), which is the declaration of holiness (*taqdīs*) and incomparability (*tanzīh*), to take place. God says: **Glorify the Name of thy Lord, the Most High.**[2] It is the manifestation-site of true existence at the levels of determination. The measuring out gives the scale for each level in respect of its rightful due and worth according to the standards of perfection and beauty. If you understood the measuring, you would truly experience the disclosure of the verse: **No disproportion dost thou see in the All-Merciful's creation.**[3]

The measuring out, therefore, is the divine mercy by virtue of which it is possible for the non-eternal to know the eternal. He gives the levels of existence their uncreated reality, and so He manifests therein through what He deposits in them. This is why it has been said that "Within the realm of possibility, there is nothing more wondrous than what actually is" (*laysa fī*

1 Q Aʿlā 87:1-3.
2 Q Aʿlā 87:1.
3 Q Mulk 67:3.

al-imkān aḥsan mimmā kān). This depositing occurs without indwelling (*ḥulūl*) or unification (*ittiḥād*), because indwelling and unification requires for there to be a duality in existence, and that is impossible because there is no existence except for the Existentiator of existence (*wājid al-wujūd*). One of al-Iskandarī's aphorisms reads,

"How far apart is the one who seeks proof through God from the one who seeks proof for God! The one who seeks proof through God acknowledges the due that he owes, and affirms the matter by reference to its original existence. One seeks proof for Him only because one has not reached Him. Otherwise, when was it that He became absent, such that one would need to seek proof for Him? And when was it that He became distant, such that one would need to follow the tracks of created things to find him?"

Were it not for the measuring out, there would be no descent and all would remain level. Creation would have no access to direct knowledge of God, and it would not be appropriate for them in any case since they would have no affinity for it. Direct knowledge of God is inextricably linked with direct knowledge of existence, which is commensurate with one's direct knowledge of existent things.

Know also that existence is found in the disclosure-site of that which exists through it, whether it be uncreated or created, universal or particular. From the intermarriage of all that we have told you here may emerge things that cannot be circumscribed by the circle of comprehensiveness, although for the People of Certitude they are circumscribed by the sphere of the noble Muḥammadan Mīm, may God bless its master. It is the secret that flows from existence (*al-wujūd*) to the existent (*al-mawjūd*):

Al-mawjūd = ***al-wujūd*** + M, the Muḥammadan Mīm.

According to the People of Lights, the numerical value of the letter Mīm is forty; so there are forty levels of descents and disclosure-sites of measuring, from the nondelimited unspoken unseen realm to the disclosure-site of the human being.

From the perspective of divine power (*qudra*), the measuring is the forms of possible things within the entities, so that the world may become known. From the perspective of the Powerful (*al-Qādir*), the measuring is that through which the knower is known. Thus, the measuring is a manifestation through nonmanifestation; He manifested the measuring in order for the power and the Powerful to become nonmanifest.

Now, you must be careful not to mix up the concepts of measuring-out and descent (*tanazzul*), although some masters did use the terms interchangeably, for we should give each technical term its proper due. Therefore you should know, dear wayfarer, that the descent becomes manifest through the measuring. For were it not for the measuring, there would be no descents or ascensions. Likewise, the measuring can be seen in the disclosure of the descent, for were it not for the descent, the measuring would not be grasped. The measuring therefore is the scale of descent, and the descent is the manifestation of the measuring.

It was through the secret of this measuring that God's folk expressed their bewilderment in the sublime Essence by reference to names such as Mayyā and Laylā in their poems and ecstatic utterances. As you see, both these names end with the letter Alif, upon which the motions (*ḥarakāt*) of existence are posited; for it is impossible to add vowels (*ḥarakāt*) to the Alif, and they can only be posited for it. Laylā (ليلى) ends with the *alif maqṣūra* (ى), the "confined Alif," which is an allusion to incapacity and the holding-back of aspiration from reaching the hallowed ground of the supreme reality. Mayyā (ميا) is an allusion to the station of "You are as You have praised Yourself," because of how the Alif of Measuring at its end is perfectly straight.

The Basmala

God says: **I swear by the places where the stars descend! And truly it is a magnificent oath, if you but knew. Truly it is a Noble Quran in a Book concealed. None touch it, save those made pure, a revelation from the Lord of the worlds.**[1]

Know that in reality, the world is none other than the Holy Qur'ān, whose stars descend in concealed places, and whose stars are numbered, and whose letter-descents are inscribed. It has three aspects, corresponding to the three worlds. In the World of Invincibility it is concealed, touched by **those made pure** of all but the Real, chosen by the Real for the presence of approval and ultimate contentment. He called them **those made pure** (*muṭahharūn*), not "those who made themselves pure" (*mutaṭahhirūn*), for they played no part in it with the presence. They are pure, perfected, and complete, and the ultimate contentment of God is upon them.

Then there is the **Book inscribed (*marqūm*), witnessed by those brought nigh;**[2] this witnessing reflects back upon their states as well as their bodies, and so to look upon them is a mercy. God says: **Thou dost recognize in their faces the splendor of bliss.**[3]

1 Q Wāqi'a 56:75-80.
2 Q Muṭaffifīn 83:20-21.
3 Q Muṭaffifīn 83:24.

Then there is the **Book written out (*masṭūr*) on parchment outspread,**[1] the parchment of this outspread existence, whose words are endless: **Say, "If the sea were ink for the Words of my Lord, the sea would be exhausted before the Words of my Lord were exhausted, even if We brought the like thereof to replenish it."**[2] This is why this existential cosmos is in constant expansion.

It is related that our master ʿAlī, may God ennoble his countenance, said: "The entire Qurʾān is collected in the Fātiḥa, and the Fātiḥa in the basmala, and the basmala in the Bāʾ; and the secret of the Bāʾ is the dot, and I am the dot." Therefore the disciple must learn how the basmala descends from the spiritual world to the physical world. If he is to master this science, he must understand something about the secrets of the dots of the Bāʾ, the Nūn of *al-Raḥmān*, and the Yāʾ of *al-Raḥīm*.

Let us begin with the Bāʾ of the basmala. Know, dear wayfarer, that the Bāʾ of the basmala is the disclosure-site of the door to the City of Knowledge. We may say that through it, the worshipper becomes distinct from the Worshipped, for it contains the secret of the Alif. When the Bāʾ enters into the word *ism*, "name," the Alif of Power (*alif al-qudra*) becomes hidden, and the Bāʾ becomes a substitute for the Hamza of Power. And since the Bāʾ is set in motion by a vowel (*ḥaraka*), this means that there is existentiation. The Bāʾ thus comes to contain the secret of the three worlds: a disclosure of spiritual-letter, invin-

1 Q Ṭūr 52:2-3.
2 Q Kahf 18:109.

cible-dot, and physical-vowel. The divine power is veiled by manifestation in its nonmanifestation, for Divinity rejects duality. God says: **Truly God forgives not that any partner be ascribed unto Him, but He forgives what is less than that for whomsoever He will.**[1] Thus we find that the Alif is manifest despite being affixed to the Bā' in the disclosure-site of **Read in the Name of thy Lord Who created,**[2] because Lordship accepts the additional presence of servitude. If not for the manifestation of the Alif, there would be no form to see. This is the station of the hadith, "I saw my Lord in the form of a beardless youth." It was in this disclosure-site that the Confidant of God asked to see his Lord: **"My Lord, show me, that I might look upon Thee."**[3] Note that he did not say, "My God," as the Israelites did when they said, **"Show us God openly."**[4] They were unwittingly asking for none other than their destruction, for Divinity **spares not, nor leaves behind,**[5] while Lordship allows servitude to subsist. This is why the Alif accepts the Bā' in **Read in the Name of thy Lord Who created.**

And because of the secret and magnificence of this disclosure, entry to the presence is through the door of the dot under the Bā'. Sidi al-Ghawth Abū Madyan, may God sanctify his secret, used to say of this, "I never saw anything without seeing the dot of the Bā' written upon it."

1 Q Nisā' 4:48.
2 Q 'Alaq 96:1.
3 Q A'rāf 7:143.
4 Q Nisā' 4:153.
5 Q Muddaththir 74:28.

Know also, dear disciple, may God assist you in attaining all that is good, that each letter of B-S-M (*bismi*) is a triangle in the image of the disclosure-site of the worlds. The Bā' comprises *Bā', Alif, Hamza*; the Sīn comprises *Sīn, Yā', Nūn*; and the Mīm comprises *Mīm, Yā', Mīm*. This is the tether of the celestial mount at this disclosure-site, because the basmala in the mirror of the spiritual realm (*malakūt*) is a triangle composed of the Bā' of *bismi*, the Nūn of *al-Raḥmān*, and the Yā' of *al-Raḥīm*. In the disclosure-site of the sensory realm, it casts a shadow when the sun of manifestation shines upon it; and that is the cubical basmala, an upper triangle along with its shadow. Thus the Blessed Ka'ba is the disclosure-site of the basmala, inasmuch as the earth is the disclosure-site of the book of existence.

The proof of what we have just said is found in the authentic hadith in which the Prophet ﷺ said to 'Ā'isha, "Were it not that your people are still too near the Age of Ignorance, I would order them to bring down the Ka'ba, and then *I would put back into it what was taken out of it*, and build it directly upon the ground, and give it two doors, one on the east and another on the west, in line with the foundations of Abraham."[1] Another narration has, "'Ā'isha, were it not that you people are newly converted from unbelief, I would reduce the Ka'ba and give it two doors, one for the people to enter and another for them to exit." So it is now the disclosure-site of the basmala and its shadow; yet if its construction were perfected, it would be a tri-

1 Bukhārī, *Ṣaḥīḥ*, Kitāb al-Ḥajj, #1586.

angle, and its treasures and secrets would become manifest.

Here you might ask: how can the basmala be the secret of union? How can I make it into a bridge to carry me over the ocean of separation?

Here it must be made clear that the lordly mentoring Shaykh is not merely someone who describes to you the disclosure-sites of the spiritual world or the secrets of Invincibility; he is the one who can make them descend to the physical world and the sensory realm, as the Companions experienced with the Chosen Prophet ﷺ when Gabriel came to them in the form of a man with very white clothes and very black hair, with no trace of travel visible upon him despite his being unknown to them all. Then the Chosen Prophet told them that he was Gabriel, who had come to teach them their religion. This is the nature of the prophetic inheritance.

My answer to you, then, is that by the grace of the Lord, we have made the journey easy to traverse, by virtue of this hundred years of which I am the Renewer and the Seal; and this is a grace which we will not conceal: **And as for the blessing of thy Lord, proclaim!**[1] God says, **And Our Word unto a thing, when We desire it, is only to say to it, "Be!" and it is.**[2] It is being within being within being, and so on, to an end known only to our Lord: **the ultimate end is unto thy Lord.**[3] The basmala of the Chosen Prophet is the origin, for he is the gemstone of the

1 Q Ḍuḥā 93:11.

2 Q Naḥl 16:40.

3 Q Najm 53:42.

seal, and from him branches the basmala of every station of prophethood and messengerhood, such as the basmala of Solomon, peace be upon him: **Verily, it is from Solomon and verily it is, 'In the Name of God, the All-Merciful, the Ever-Merciful...'**[1] Solomon was the disclosure-site of **In the Name of God, the All-Merciful, the Ever-Merciful.** The same is true of the basmala of Noah, upon him be peace: **He said, "Embark upon it. In the Name of God be its coursing and its mooring. Truly my Lord is Forgiving, Merciful."**[2] It is a basmala within a basmala within a basmala. The clearer your witnessing and discernment becomes, and the stronger your worship through detachment, the nearer you will draw to the wellspring of sanctity in the Alif.

Consider this diagram to understand this better:

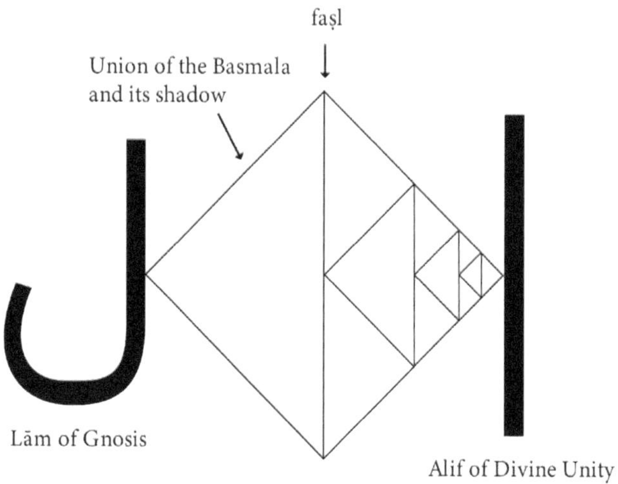

1 Q Naml 27:30.
2 Q Hūd 11:41.

The Level of the Alif

The first disclosure of the dot was the Alif, when it flowed and inclined away from its center and loved to be known; for it had no way to come out until it was uttered. Thus the Alif manifested as the locus of immanent transcendence: **Nothing is as His like,**[1] and so even in transcendence the *Ka*, "as," of immanence is affirmed. Thus the Alif came forth, transcendent beyond hollowness, circularity, or curvature; and from it came all the other letters, for the letters are nothing but the Alif made immanent by circularity and curvature. The Alif is annihilated by His name, and subsists by His Essence, and in this level it is called a Tā', or a Ṭā', or whatever other letter.

God's folk see the Alif in the letters without being prevented from seeing it by the circularity or curvature. As for the common people, these qualities prevent them from seeing the Alif, which is why they object to the humanity in the disclosure-site of elite distinction, which is why they say, "**What ails this Messenger, who eats food and walks in the markets? Why is there not an angel sent down unto him to be a warner with him?**"[2] The crucial thing here is that you learn how to banish the form and witness the Alif of All-Mercy flowing by the attrib-

1 Q Shūrā 42:11.
2 Q Shūrā 25:7.

ute of divine measure through the letters of creation. So it was that the beloved Prophet ﷺ could see the Gabrielic attribute in the angel Gabriel when he came to him in the form of Diḥya al-Kalbī. He did not hold him to a specific form, but would receive the revelation from him in whatever form he came to him. Likewise, the disciple must see union in the letters of the disciples, so that he learns how to show them due courtesy, for they are the nearest descent of the Alif, and so their nearness is more manifest and vivid.

The level of the Alif here is the disclosure-site of the divine measuring, and the Breath that embraces the divine multiplicity from the levels, the names, and their dictates. You must therefore give preference to existence over nonexistence in them, because it is by the Alif that you flow through separation, and it is from it that you come to grasp the degree of faith in the unseen that is measured out for creation, so that in each person the measure of union and separation is manifested.

The Strings of Measuring

It is through the measuring (*taqdīr*) that the All-Powerful Measurer (*Qadīr*) is known; and if not for the measuring, no one would be guided to the All-Powerful Measurer. God says: **Glorify the Name of thy Lord...Who measured out, then guided.**[1] By the measuring, the wayfarers are guided to the eternal presence; and from its manifestations, they venerate the Alif of All-Mercy which embraces all existent things.

Upon the strings of measuring, the perfected ones play their tune. In this station, the Shaykh of our Shaykh Sidi al-ʿAlawī said, may God sanctify his spirit, "The root is in my hand, and the branch grows." Their essences are the locus of eternity and the meeting-place of existence and nonexistence. They bring together the opposites without changing either side. Every glance, move, and word from them stirs all of existence into motion. Their tears are nourishing rain. God says, **Neither Heaven nor earth wept for them, nor were they granted respite.**[2] The circles of existence subsist through their reality and are connected to them, for they are the locus of the divine gaze, the focal point of the descent of *baraka*, and the wellspring of the influence of transmission.

1 Q Aʿlā 87:1-3.

2 Q Dukhān 44:29.

The Mediator has mastery of the Alif of the All-Merciful, and with it he strums the strings of existence, which are his descents: the disciples. This is why each of them, in this station, must know the note of their existence, and thereby know the reality of their souls in this station, their role in the world, and what measuring of the All-Powerful flows in them. The wayfarer must strive in this way until he attains clarity, so that he may avoid the discourtesy of encroaching upon the string of another. He must identify the string of divine measuring that flows through him in the moment—is it the measuring of the names, the presences, the intimate discourses, or the service of the masters?

On the day of Badr, the Messenger of God ﷺ asked his Companions their opinion on what should be done with the captives. Abū Bakr said, "Messenger of God, they are your people, your kinsmen. Spare them and show them mercy, and it may be that God will relent to them." ʿUmar said, "Messenger of God, they denied you and drove you out. Strike them down!" ʿAbd Allāh ibn Rawāḥa said, "Messenger of God, fill a pit with firewood and throw them in, then set them ablaze." Horrified by this, ʿAbbās cried, "Woe betide you!" The Messenger of God ﷺ went inside without giving any reply. The people wondered among themselves whose advice he would follow, each of them giving their own predictions. Finally the Messenger of God ﷺ came out to them and said, "God causes the hearts of some men to melt for His sake until they are softer than milk; and He causes the hearts of other men to harden for His sake until they are firmer than rock. Abū Bakr, truly you are like Abraham, who said, '**Whosoever follows me, he is of me. And whosoever disobeys me, surely Thou art Forgiving, Merciful.**'[1] And you are like Jesus, who said, '**If Thou punishest them, they are indeed Thy servants, but if Thou forgivest them, then indeed Thou art the Mighty, the Wise.**'[2] 'Umar, truly you are like Noah, who said, '"**My Lord, leave not a single disbeliever to dwell upon the earth.**'[3] And you are like Moses, who said, '**Our Lord! Blot out their wealth and harden their hearts, so that they will not believe till they see the painful punishment.**'"[4]

Observe how the Chosen Prophet displayed the disclosure-site of divine measuring that flowed through both al-Ṣiddīq and al-Fārūq. You too must strive in this station until you attain clarity regarding your affair and ascertain what your portion of the Presence is. God says, **There is none among us, but that he has a known station.**[5]

1 Q Ibrāhīm 14:36.
2 Q Mā'ida 5:118.
3 Q Nūḥ 71:26.
4 Q Yūnus 10:88.
5 Q Ṣāffāt 37:164.

The Melody of Existence

Know, dear wayfarer, that every vicegerent whom God appoints on the earth is the Adam of Existence. When he comes to know himself through himself, and sees the names flowing through his essence, his essence becomes the root of existence. No sooner does he realize this than he plays, in the spiritual dominion of the All-Merciful with the singularity of his innermost secret, the melody of the All-Powerful Measurer upon the ether of the waves of the divine measuring. This melody is heard by the ears of the hearts, which prostrate before him in humility and deference. God says, **Hast thou not considered that unto God prostrates whosoever is in the heavens and whosoever is on the earth, the sun, the moon, the stars, the mountains, the trees, and the beasts, and many among mankind? But for many the punishment has come due. Whomsoever God disgraces, none can ennoble. Truly God does whatsoever He will.**[1]

However, when the spirits descended to the sensory world, and the fragrance of the olive was infused with the shapes of clay, and many years passed and they departed from the secure city, they forgot the covenant of the vicegerent of **the most**

1 Q Ḥajj 22:18.

beautiful stature and were reduced to **the lowest of the low.**[1] Then those destined for the Gardens of Nearness encountered those who could remind them of the meeting, who laid the hand of the Covenant upon them so that they recalled the pledge of "**Yea, we bear witness**",[2] and saw the Light of the divine measuring flowing in their hearts with the eye of certainty. They remembered the melody of purity and faithfulness, the secret of existence and eternity. And so they rejoice and exult, and dance whenever they yearn for their homeland and ache for the meeting.

Sidi Abū Madyan al-Ghawth said, may God sanctify his spirit:

When the spirits tremble with yearning for the meeting,
The bodies dance, O you who knows not the meaning!

My son, have you not seen how the caged bird,
When it sings of home, yearns for what it sings of?

With its song it gives release to what its heart harbors,
And it becomes enraptured, in body and in spirit.

It dances between the bars, yearning to be reunited,
And its song drives intelligent men to delirium.

1 Q Tīn 95:5.
2 Q Aʿrāf 7:172.

Such are the spirits of the lovers, my son,
Stirred by yearning for the sublime land;

Shall we tell them to be patient in the midst of their aching?
Can the one who has witnessed such meaning be patient?

VI – Prophethood (*Nubuwwa*)

About what do they question one another?
About the Great Tiding.

The Everlasting Presence
(*ḥaḍrat al-khulūd*)

Dear disciple, we are at the door of the presence of the Alif's contact, which we call the everlasting presence. It is named this because none of the beautiful company of Prophets and Messengers who enter its bounds would ever deny the primordial covenant. God says: **It is not for any human being, God having given him the Book, judgment, and prophethood, to then say to the people, "Be servants of me instead of God." Rather, "Be sages, from having taught the Book and from having studied."**[1]

Know also that the Hidden Alif into whose esoteric meanings we are presently delving comprises three levels: the level of prophethood (*nubuwwa*), the level of messengerhood (*risāla*), and the level of sainthood (*wilāya*).

The everlasting presence is the presence of spiritual vigil in the company of the Lord, and following the footsteps of the mentoring Shaykh in all matters, great and small. For the Alif is a straight path that will not tolerate any crookedness in the disciple's thought, nor any shakiness in his caprices. If you would grasp and walk this path, you must be prepared to surrender yourself entirely. Yet you must not deem yourself pure

1 Q Āl ʿImrān 3:79.

and say, "I have achieved self-surrender:" **Hast thou not seen those who deem themselves pure? Rather, it is God Who purifies whomsoever He will.**[1] Instead you must always view yourself critically and belittle your state. True self-surrender means to nullify your lesser intellect completely and renounce all claims to strength and transformative power; for your intellect can only take you further away from God—we seek His refuge from that!

Self-surrender comes from you first, and then afterwards come the proofs and signs to reassure your heart. A sacred hadith says: "When the servant draws a hand's span nearer to Me, I draw an arm's length nearer to Him. When he draws an arm's length nearer to Me, I draw a fathom nearer to him. When he comes walking to Me, I go running to him."[2] So it begins with you, and ends with your Lord: **Truly God alters not what is in a people until they alter what is in themselves.**[3]

By God, what is the status of your delimited nonexistent intellect next to that of the intellect of the Shaykh, which is characterized with the presence of the Supreme Intellect, the mover of the divine laws? He is the heir of the all-encompassing utterances (*jawāmiʿ al-kalim*), and is able to cause pure meaning to descend into the receptacles of forms in the manner required to guide people.

1 Q Nisāʾ 4:49.
2 Bukhārī, *Ṣaḥīḥ*, Kitāb al-Tawḥīd, #7098.
3 Q Raʿd 13:11.

Enter this station without your intellect; enter it with the intellect of your Shaykh. Have you not heard the words of the Chosen Prophet ﷺ, "Most of the people of Paradise are fools"? The everlasting presence bars entry to people with delimited intellects. I said of this in a poem:

To me, ascend by descending,
Keep every intellect at bay,

This is the root of roots,
To understand what I say.

Reflect, may God have mercy on you, on how when God's Prophet Jonah left his people when they refused to believe in God, God tried him with the manifold darkness of the ocean, the night, and the belly of the whale. This was only because the station of prophethood accepts nothing other than what the Presence dictates. God says: **And [remember] Dhu'l-Nūn, when he went away in anger, and thought We had no power over him. Then he cried out in the darkness, "There is no god but Thee! Glory be to Thee! Truly I have been among the wrongdoers." So We answered him, and saved him from grief. Thus do We save the believers.**[1]

So the everlasting presence begins with total self-surrender based upon acquiescence and the nullification of the delimited

1 Q Anbiyā' 21:87-88.

intellect. The one who enters it with his own mind will squander the door of prophethood just as it was squandered by the companions of Khālid b. Sinān, upon him be peace, when they failed to acquiesce to his words. Ibn ʿAbbās, may God be pleased with him, related that a man of the tribe of ʿAbs named Khālid b. Sinān said to his people, "I will extinguish the eternal fire for you." A man of his people named ʿUmāra b. Ziyād said to him, "By God, you have only ever told us the truth, Khālid. But what is this about the eternal fire? Do you really claim you can put it out?" So they went together along with thirty other men of his people, until they came to the fire, which emitted from a cleft in a mountain of volcanic rock called Ashjaʿ Tract. Khālid drew a line for them and told them to sit inside it. "If I am late in returning to you," he told them, "do not call me by my name."

The fire came roaring out of the cleft like a stampede of wild horses. Khālid faced it head on, beating it back with his staff and saying, "Get back, get back! Every offering will be delivered! The goat-herder's son claimed that I would not come back out with my garments unburned!" Then he disappeared inside the cleft. After a long time had passed with no sign of him, ʿUmāra ibn Ziyād said, "By God, if he were still alive he would have come out by now." They said, "Then call him by his name." Some of them objected that he had expressly forbidden them from doing so, but they called his name anyway. He came out to them at once, holding his head in his hands. "Didn't I tell you not to call me by my name?", he said. "By God, you have killed me, so bury me. If some donkeys should come your way, one of them with a severed tail, then dig me up, and you will find me alive." So they buried him.

Later some donkeys passed by, one of which had a severed tail. The people took this as a sign that they should exhume Khālid as he had instructed, but 'Umāra b. Ziyād objected saying, "We cannot have the folk of Muḍar going around saying that we dig up our dead! By God, we must never exhume him."

Khālid had told them that he had left two tablets in the care of his wife which they should consult in times of uncertainty, whereupon they would find guidance. He also instructed that these tablets should not be touched by a menstruating woman. So they went to his wife and asked for the tablets, and she brought them out, but she was menstruating, and all the knowledge inscribed upon them faded away.

Abū Yūnus related on the authority of Simāk b. Ḥarb that the Prophet ﷺ was asked about Khālid, and replied, "That was a prophet whose people squandered him." Simāk also related that the son of Khālid b. Sinān once visited the Prophet ﷺ, who said to him, "Welcome, my brother's son!"

Ḥākim declared this narration to be authentic according to the criteria of Bukhārī and Muslim. He also noted that the story of Khālid b. Sinān's death was related in different ways, and that he heard from several trusted narrators of al-Andalus that between their homeland and Qayrawān there was a sea in the middle of which stood a tall mountain that no one ever climbed. Their journeys by sea took them close by this mountain, and they had seen at the top a cave in which sat a man with his legs drawn up, swaddled in white wool, his head resting on his hands as though he were asleep, his body entirely unchanged. They told of how the locals there swore that he was Khālid b. Sinān. God knows best.[1]

1 Ḥākim, *al-Mustadrak ʿalā al-Ṣaḥīḥayn*, K. Tawārīkh al-Mutaqaddimīn min al-Anbiyāʾ waʾl-Mursalīn, #4173. The versions given by Ṭabarānī and Ibn Shabba were also consulted to translate this passage.

The Great Tiding

God says: **About what do they question one another? About the Great Tiding, regarding which they differ. Nay, but they will know! Then indeed they will know!**[1]

Dear disciple, we are currently concerned with the everlasting presence by way of the core of prophethood. You should know that the prophethood about which we are speaking is the prophethood of sainthood (*nubuwwat al-wilāya*). If you ask whether sainthood for its part has prophethood, the answer is yes, it has both prophethood and messengerhood, but this prophethood does not make you a prophet. It is a prophethood of inspiration (*nubuwwat ilhām*), not legislation (*tashrīʿ*); it does not involve any lawmaking, but only knowledge of the station. So that you are not confused about any of this, let us begin by elucidating the station of prophethood, so that the image may become clearer for you.

God says: **Muhammad is not the father of any man among you; rather, he is the Messenger of God and the Seal of the prophets. And God is Knower of all things.**[2] The two *Ṣaḥīḥ* collections relate how Abū Ḥāzim said, "I sat with Abū Hurayra for five years and heard him relate how the Prophet ﷺ said, 'The

1 Q Naba' 78:1-5.
2 Q Aḥzāb 33:40.

Israelites were ruled by the prophets; whenever a prophet died, another would replace him. Yet there will be no prophet after me.'"[1] The prophethood meant in this hadith is the prophethood of laws; after the Messenger ﷺ, there would be no other lawgiving prophet. Yet it is authentically narrated that at the end of time, God's Prophet Jesus Christ will descend, may peace be upon him. From the hadith, we know that he will not descend with the prophethood of laws, for that station was sealed with the Beloved Messenger ﷺ. Rather, he will descend with the station of sainthood, which is why he will not lead the prayer, but stand behind the imam.

The prophethood of laws, then, came to an end and was sealed by our master Muḥammad ﷺ. From here on out we shall speak about the station of the prophethood of sainthood, not the prophethood of the prophets; for that is another science altogether, called the science of the presences (*ʿilm al-ḥaḍarāt*).

Know, may the Lord give you the grace to know Him, that the Tiding (*nabaʾ*) is a veridical address, a lordly description, and a divine spirit. It flows from the door of God's words, **The Raiser of degrees, the Possessor of the Throne, He casts the Spirit from His Command upon whomsoever He will among His servants to warn of the Day of the Meeting.**[2] The Raiser of Degrees is one of the disclosures of the Singular Alif from the door of prophethood, which casts the commanding spirit upon whomsoever He will of His servants, who receive the disclosure

1 Muslim, *Ṣaḥīḥ*, K. al-Imāra, #1842a.

2 Q Ghāfir 40:15.

along with the tiding. For if the inblowing and the casting were not in the form of a tiding, they would not be intelligible. The inblowing must have affinity with the preparedness of the vessel into which it is inblown. God says: **Thus have We revealed unto thee a Spirit from Our Command. Thou knewest not what scripture was, nor faith. But We made it a Light whereby We guide whomsoever We will among Our servants. Truly thou dost guide unto a straight path.**[1] The Light of instruction bequeaths the book and faith; that is, knowledge of laws and certainty in the rewards and acts of nearness that they convey to one. This is the disclosure that accompanies the tiding.

Consider the story of the Prophet John, upon him be peace, when the Israelites wanted to kill him, and split the tree in which he was hiding. The stories tell us that when he cried out, God revealed to him, "If you do not cease, I shall wipe your name from the registry of prophets." The folk of knowledge explain that this means, "I shall lift from you the path of tidings, and give you things through pure disclosure; and disclosure can only conform to your preparedness, through which experiential perception can occur."

So the meaning of the verse is that the purpose of the tiding is **to warn of the Day of the Meeting**, which has been interpreted to mean the day of the meeting between creation and the Creator. That applies to the case of those who are oblivious of the Light of truth, for they confine the Real to a certain time for

1 Q Shūrā 42:52.

the beatific vision and meeting. As for the People of Light, they consider that the subject of the verb in **to warn of the Day of the Meeting** is the presence of lordship. For the people of sensory vision, the warner is the Prophet; for the people of inner vision, the warner is the Lord of the Prophet. God says: **You did not slay them, but God slew them, and thou threwest not when thou threwest, but God threw.**[1]

Prophethood for other than the Prophets, then, is a kind of prophethood viewed through the glass of sainthood; a sainthood of inspiration, or, if you will, a lunar prophethood which draws its Light from the solar prophethood of the Prophet.

The prophethood that concerns us here is one of the stations of the Alif of Divine Unity, which turns in the orbit of Supreme Sainthood, unending because it is founded on the secret of sainthood, and the subsistence of sainthood is founded on the Name of Majesty. One of the names of God is the Friend, *al-Walī*; God says, **God is the Friend of those who believe.**[2] But His names do not include the Prophet, *al-Nabī*, or the Messenger, *al-Rasūl*, which is why prophethood and messengerhood have come to an end. As for the prophethood of sainthood, it is everlasting because it is one of the levels of sainthood, and one of the two bows of its length.

1 Q Anfāl 8:17.
2 Q Baqara 2:257.

The Prophethood of Sainthood

Know, may the Lord alert you and guide you to the path of eternity, that making contact with the Hidden Alif occurs through the blessing of the secret of sainthood, which has a liminal position in the journey through the station of eternity. It is the unique pearl that most of creation are unable to understand. Indeed, because of the humble situations in which it manifests in the lowliest levels of servanthood, such as sickness and hunger, most of those searching for the path scarcely pay it any mind. Some of them even reject it and fight it, purely because of their ignorance of its rank and tremendous secret.

In our age, most Muslims—**save those upon whom thy Lord has Mercy**[1]—pay no heed to the realm of sainthood. Some of them think it is heresy, others that it is fakery, others that it is superstition, others still that it is mere philosophy. Even among the few who are chosen by the Lord to recognize the tremendousness of this matter, fewer still of them give it its proper due. Most of them are motivated by the hope that they will inherit it from the predecessors, or the presumption that they already possess it and are among its elites.

1 Q Hūd 11:119.

You are in a station that heaven and earth struggle to bear, and the two weighty kingdoms of the jinn and mankind covet. Know that the secret of sainthood is manifest in the Hidden Alif through two tremendous stations, namely the prophethood of sainthood and the messengerhood of sainthood—for indeed sainthood does possess prophethood and messengerhood, not in the sense of establishing new laws, but in the sense of knowledge and practice upon the insight of the everlasting station.

The station of prophethood was indeed sealed by the Beloved Prophet ﷺ. When the essence of Muḥammad ibn ʿAbd Allāh became manifest, the circle was completed and the last became one with the first. He ﷺ said, "I was the first of the Prophets to be created, and the last to be sent."[1] He was the spirit blown into Adam, and the cosmos came into being through him and for him. Paradise was created for his loved ones, Hell for his enemies. The hadith of Jābir, may God be pleased with him, is a fulsome and satisfying answer for anyone who wishes to be in the know. It is related that Jābir asked the Prophet ﷺ about the first thing God created. He replied.

"It was the Light of your Prophet, Jābir. God created it, then created within it all that is good, and after that created all things. When He created it, He placed it front of Him in the Station of Proximity for twelve thousand years. Then He divided it into four parts. He created the Throne from one part, the Pedestal from another, and the Throne-bearers and attendants of the

1 Ibn ʿAdī, *al-Kāmil*, vol. 3, p. 1209.

Pedestal from another. He placed the fourth part in the Station of Love for twelve thousand years, then divided it into four parts. He created the Pen from one part, the Tablet from another, and the Garden from another. He placed the fourth part in the Station of Fear for twelve thousand years, then divided it into four parts. He created the angels from one part, the sun from another, and the moon and planets from another. He placed the fourth part in the Station of Hope for twelve thousand years, then divided it into four parts. He created the intellect from one part, knowledge and wisdom from another, and inerrancy (*ʿiṣma*) and divine success (*tawfīq*) from another. He placed the fourth part in the Station of Shame for twelve thousand years, then looked at it, and the Light began to drip with sweat. From it poured one hundred and twenty-four thousand drops of Light, and from each drop God created the spirit of a Prophet or a Messenger. Then the spirits of the Prophets began to breathe, and God created from their breaths the saints, the felicitous, the martyrs, and all the obedient believers till the Day of Judgment. The Throne and the Pedestal are thus from my Light. The Cherubim are from my Light. The spiritual beings (*rūḥāniyyūn*) and the angels are from my Light. The Garden with all its bliss is from my Light. The angels and the seven heavens are from my Light. The sun, the moon, and the planets are from my Light. The intellect and divine success are from my Light. The spirits of the Messengers and the Prophets are from my Light. The martyrs, the felicitous, and the righteous are products of my Light. Then God created twelve thousand veils, and placed my Light, which is the fourth part, within each veil for one thousand years. These are the stations of servanthood (*ʿubūdiyya*), tranquility (*sakīna*), patience (*ṣabr*), truthfulness (*ṣidq*), and certitude (*yaqīn*). God immersed that Light in every veil for a thousand years. Then when He brought it out of the veils, He instilled it upon the earth, such that it lit up everything that lies between the east and the west, like a lamp on a dark night. Then God created Adam from the earth, and instilled that Light in his brow. Then it passed to Seth, and so on from one pure man to the next, one good man to the next, until God passed it to the loins of ʿAbd Allāh b. ʿAbd al-Muṭṭalib, and from him to the womb of my mother Āmina bint Wahb. Then He brought me forth into this world and appointed me the Master of the Messengers, the Seal of the Prophets, and the Mercy to the Worlds. That was how the creation of your Prophet began, Jābir.'"[1]

So today, sainthood is the door to enter the city of prophetic knowledge, for it is everlasting and prevailing because it is divinely supported; God is the Friend, *al-Walī*. There will be no other Law after the Prophet ﷺ, and even when Jesus Christ descends at the end of time, he will descend as a manifestation of sainthood beneath the Law of the Chosen Prophet, a follower, not a leader.

You might ask how exactly the station of sainthood's prophethood functions, and whether it involves revelation or not, and

1 See Suyūṭī, *al-Ḥāwī li'l-fatāwī*, vol. 1, p. 323.

whether new legislation can be known through it or not. Know, then, that the station of sainthood's prophethood is taken from the wellspring of sainthood in your era. It is the Alif that flows through the letters of creation, the lordly source of the divine replenishment that shapes existence. It is the dot of the Bā' of the basmala, from which the Qur'ān of existence is disclosed.

Know also that revelation is not restricted to the Prophets and Messengers alone, for it is also possible for others to receive it. **God revealed to the mother of Moses: So We revealed to the mother of Moses, "Nurse him. But if you fear for him, then cast him into the river, and fear not, nor grieve. Surely We shall bring him back to you and make him one of the messengers."**[1] This is the revelation of inspiration, not of laws. It is revelation by which you grasp the meaning of the Law of the Chosen Prophet and take it directly from the Lawgiver, unlike how the common people take it, one dead person from another. You recognize the purpose and the secret of everything the Chosen Prophet did, said, or approved. You become one of the people of knowledge, for whom the fish in the sea and the ants in the rocks send up prayers for forgiveness. This is far from the common misperception that knowledge is a matter of memorization. For us, such a person is merely a carrier, not a knower. A hadith says, "May God have mercy on a servant who hears my words and remembers them, then passes them on to another who did not hear them. Many a man carries knowledge he does

1 Q Qaṣaṣ 28:7.

not understand, and many a man carries knowledge to another who understands it better than he does."[1]

1 Ḥākim, *Mustadrak*, K. al-'Ilm, #303.

The Supreme Intellect

Dear wayfarer, in this station we would like you to attain the esoteric realities of existence. In order for you to achieve this in the station of prophethood, you must adorn yourself with the disclosure-site of the Supreme Intellect (*al-ʿaql al-akbar*), which flows with the Supreme Light by which veils are rent asunder and the darkness of the delimited intellect is banished.

The disciple's thought is rooted in ignorance, for it is founded on the disclosures of the forms of possible things, and so transfers from physical to spiritual; from form to form. Yet pure meaning is obviously higher than form. This is why in this station one must adorn oneself with the intellect of prophethood. This intellect has many names; some call it the Supreme Tablet, others the First Intellect, others the Supreme Spirit.

A man asked the Prophet ﷺ if he should tie his camel and trust in God, or let it go free and trust in God. The Prophet ﷺ replied, "Tie it (*iʿqil-hā*) and trust in God."[1] This hadith shows the value of the intellect in every child of Adam. For in reality, the intellects of the children of Adam all have the power of the intellect of all existence from the moment of **"Am I not your Lord?"**[2] until the Lote Tree of the Furthest Boundary. However,

1 Tirmidhī, *Jāmiʿ*, K. Ṣifat al-Qiyāma, #2517.

2 Q Aʿrāf 7:172.

no one ever reached this aspiration except the Beloved Prophet ﷺ, who brought back a book containing all that was and all that shall be.

As for the intellect of the people of the herebelow, its object can be nothing more than conjecture and delimited thought. God says, **They follow naught but conjecture and that which their souls desire.**[1] Then they apply these sensory delimited forms to the unseen, and so loftiness appears to them as nothing more than positional height, and nearness and farness appear to them as nothing more than spatial distance, and so on for other pure meanings. This is because the physical world has six directions, while the spiritual world has only two.

As for the intellect of prophethood, it perceives the unseen according to the reality of the station of witnessing in the rings of existence. For it possesses the secret of the flow, and so it perceives each reality in the ring of its existence, and grasps every level and its descents, dictates, and branches. During his night journey, the Beloved Prophet ﷺ tied the celestial mount to a ring to which the other Prophets tied their mounts. That ring was the ring of the cord (*ʿiqāl*) of the perceptions of prophethood, whose location is the holy sanctuary of nonmanifestation. The Chosen Prophet ﷺ said in a long hadith, "The seven heavens, compared to the Pedestal, are like a ring thrown upon open ground; and the Throne compared to the Pedestal is like that open ground compared to the ring." Every heaven is a ring; that

1 Q Najm 53:23.

is, like a circle surrounding all that is below it. Compared to what is above it, it is like a ring thrown down in a desert; and the same difference exists between the heaven and the Pedestal, then between the Pedestal and the Throne. Every ring is a cord that ties the sciences and secrets of that heaven, to the Throne, to the Lote Tree. Nothing ties all of this except the intellect of the Prophet ﷺ.

The Spirit of Command

God says, **Your creation and your resurrection are as naught but a single soul. Truly God is Hearing, Seeing.**[1]

Know, may the Lord have mercy on you, that the Supreme Spirit descends with the perfect soul to the drinking-places (*mashārib*) of the particular souls, in order to complete their knowledge and means of drawing nearer to the presence of lordly eternity. The presence of the Supreme Spirit is the sun of existence, our master the Chosen Prophet ﷺ, and the particular souls are the circle that surrounds his blessed gemstone.

Every Prophet in his own time had the central place among his people, acting as a deputy for the Supreme Master ﷺ. All of their actions and ascensions were through the spiritual reality of the Beloved ﷺ, for they all drew replenishment from his blessed presence. An example of this is how Solomon, upon him be peace, disclosed the basmala in his own era: **She said, "O notables! Truly a noble letter has been delivered unto me. Verily, it is from Solomon and verily it/he is, 'In the Name of God, the Compassionate, the Merciful…"**[2] That is, Solomon was identical with the basmala, and through it he governed the worlds of men and jinn, and subdued the winds, mountains,

1 Q Luqmān 31:28.
2 Q Naml 27:29-30.

and birds. The same is true of Jesus, Moses, and Noah, upon them be peace; they were delegates, while the Chosen Prophet was the original. They were the deputies of the Prophet among their people, as though each of them was one of the realities of the Chosen Prophet, descended with what was right for that time and era; a deputy bearing a reality. This went on until time desired to come full circle, whereupon the Chosen Prophet became manifest in the person of Muḥammad ibn ʿAbd Allāh ﷺ.

I only spoke to you of the station of the universal soul and the particular souls in order to bring you closer to the soul of your Shaykh and your Mediator, and so that you may know that all of the blessings your Lord grants you are from the descents of your Shaykh. He is the heir of the spiritual reality of the Chosen Prophet in his time, and you are in the station of one of the Prophets. A tradition says, "The knowers of my Community are better than the Prophets of the Israelites."

Cling to your Shaykh's eminent person and impregnable grace, for he is the pure meaning of existence and the spirit's refreshment. The moon of the knowledge of prophethood will not Light up in your heart until the sun of his sainthood shines upon it.

In sum, if not for the soul of the Shaykh in his time, souls would not know any path to the world of eternity, nor any way to reach the core of the knowledge of prophethood; for he is the summary of the worlds and the index of existence. If you wish to drink from the wellspring of sainthood's prophethood, do not see anything from your soul besides the realities of your Shaykh. That is, see with his sight, and hear with his hearing, and grasp with his hand, and walk with his feet.

The Queen Bee of Spirits

Dear disciple, know that the station of prophethood in the disclosure-site of sainthood in this blessed Community may be grasped by the blessing of the queen bee of spirits and the magnet of truth, our master the Chosen Prophet ﷺ. The Prophets from the previous communities and the saints of their time all stood in the tracks of what the pre-eternal wisdom dictated for those times. Each Prophet, according to the measure of the blessing he received from the Messenger of God ﷺ, was the focal point of realities in his time, while the saints of his time drew replenishment from his periphery.

Now, since we are a middle community, which is solely by the blessing of the Beloved ﷺ, we are witnesses over all communities, for we are the periphery around the universal central point that gathers together all the affairs of the Essence. This means that all the other communities must be within the periphery of our centrality.

God says: **Thus did We make you a middle community, that you may be witnesses for mankind and that the Messenger may be a witness for you.**[1] The supreme centrality is for the Chosen Prophet ﷺ, and the periphery is for the saints of his

1 Q Baqara 2:143.

community. This periphery touches the central points of the previous communities, which is why some of our saints are Moses-like, others Jesus-like.

A tradition tells that on the day of Badr, the Messenger of God ﷺ asked his Companions their opinion on what should be done with the captives. Abū Bakr said, "Messenger of God, they are your people, your kinsmen. Spare them and show them mercy, and it may be that God will relent to them." ʿUmar said, "Messenger of God, they denied you and drove you out. Strike them down!" ʿAbd Allāh ibn Rawāḥa said, "Messenger of God, fill a pit with firewood and throw them in, then set them ablaze." Horrified by this, ʿAbbās cried, "Woe betide you!" The Messenger of God ﷺ went inside without giving any reply. The people wondered among themselves whose advice he would follow, each of them giving their own predictions. Finally the Messenger of God ﷺ came out to them and said, "God causes the hearts of some men to melt for His sake until they are softer than milk; and He causes the hearts of other men to harden for His sake until they are firmer than rock. Abū Bakr, truly you are like Abraham, who said, '**Whosoever follows me, he is of me. And whosoever disobeys me, surely Thou art Forgiving, Merciful.**'[1] **And you are like Jesus, who said, 'If Thou punishest them, they are indeed Thy servants, but if Thou forgivest them, then indeed Thou art the Mighty, the Wise.**'[2] ʿUmar, truly you are like Noah, who said, '"**My Lord, leave not a single**

1 Q Ibrāhīm 14:36.
2 Q Māʾida 5:118.

disbeliever to dwell upon the earth.'[1] And you are like Moses, who said, '**Our Lord! Blot out their wealth and harden their hearts, so that they will not believe till they see the painful punishment.'**"[2]

The Chosen Prophet is the supreme brick in the wall of the isthmus. An authentic hadith states, "The likeness of me and the Prophets before me is like that of a man who builds a house with excellent craftsmanship and beautiful artistry, except for one brick in a corner. People begin to flock around the house, admiring it and saying, 'But if only you would place the last brick!' I am that brick, and I am the Seal of Prophets."[3]

Beneath the wall is the treasure of mystical knowledge. God says: **And as for the wall, it belonged to two orphan boys in the city, and beneath it was a treasure belonging to them. Their father was righteous.**[4] The righteous father is the saint, and the two boys are prophethood and messengerhood; for every prophet or messenger begins as a saint, and his foundation always remains sainthood. In the end he wishes to return to sainthood, for as we said, sainthood is everlasting because one of the names of God is *al-Walī.* Consider how when the Prophets are at death's door, they implore God to join them with the righteous.

1 Q Nūḥ 71:26.
2 Q Yūnus 10:88.
3 Bukhārī, *Ṣaḥīḥ*, K. al-Manāqib, #3535.
4 Q Qāf 18:82.

God says: **On the Day when the hypocrites, men and women, will say to those who believe, "Wait for us that we may borrow from your Light," it will be said, "Turn back and seek a Light!" Thereupon a wall with a gate will be set down between them, the inner side of which contains mercy, and on the outer side of which lies punishment.**[1] None remain outside the wall but the people of hypocrisy. The wall symbolizes a circle, and the Sufi ritual dance of the *ḥaḍra* alludes to this. Be part of the wall, or be inside it, for its inside is the mercy of esoteric realities and the blessings of witnessing and disclosure.

This diagram may help you understand what we have said about the peripheral and central relationship between us and the previous communities:

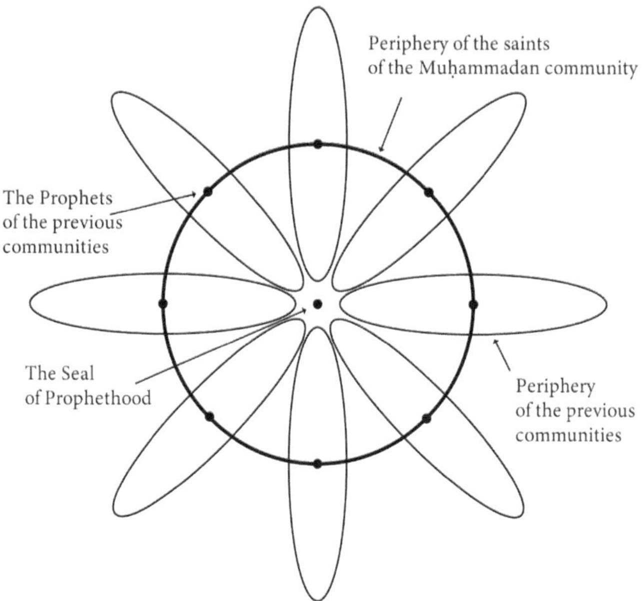

1 Q Ḥadīd 57:13.

He Sat Knee-to-Knee With Him

Know, dear disciple, may God grace you with abundant courtesy, that this hadith comprises the entire foundations of the religion. I mean, of course, the hadith narrated by al-Fārūq 'Umar b. al-Khaṭṭab, may God be pleased with him, who said:

"One day when we were with God's Messenger ﷺ, a man with very white clothing and very black hair came up to us. No mark of travel was visible on him, and none of us recognized him. He sat down knee-to-knee with the Prophet ﷺ, placed his hands on his thighs, and said: 'Tell me, Muḥammad, about submission (*islām*).' The Messenger of God ﷺ replied, 'Submission is to bear witness that there is no god but God, and that Muḥammad is God's Messenger, and to perform the ritual prayer, pay the alms tax, fast during Ramaḍān, and make the pilgrimage to the House if you are able to.' The man said, 'You have spoken the truth.' We were surprised at how he questioned him and then confirmed his reply. He said, 'Now tell me about faith (*īmān*).' He replied, 'Faith is to believe in God, His angels, His books, His messengers, and the Last Day, and to believe in the measuring out, both its good and its evil.' The man said again, 'You have spoken the truth. Now tell me about spiritual excellence (*iḥsān*).' He replied, 'Spiritual excellence is to worship God as if you see Him (*ka-annaka tarāh*), for even if you see Him not,

He sees you.' Then the man said, 'Tell me about the Hour (*sā'a*).' The Prophet replied, 'About that, he who is questioned knows no more than the questioner.' The man said, 'Then tell me of its portents.' He replied, 'The slave-girl will give birth to her mistress, and you will see barefoot, naked, destitute shepherds vying with each other in the construction of tall buildings.' Then the man went away. After I had waited a while, the Prophet said to me, 'Do you know who the questioner was, 'Umar?' I replied, 'God and His Messenger know best.' He said, 'He was Gabriel. He came to teach you your religion.'"[1]

I quoted the hadith in full for you here so that from it you may glean the courtesy (*adab*) of company in the station of prophethood, in the discourse-site of the contact of the Hidden Alif. For courtesy is everything, and it has been said, "Make your courtesy flour, and your worship salt." That is, most of your effort should be concentrated on attaining the station of courtesy, for it is the only route to sublime proximity. Another hadith says, "With good character, a servant may reach tremendous levels and splendid stations in the hereafter, even if his worship is weak. And with poor character, he may fall to the deepest depths of Hell, even if he is a devoted worshipper." Let the cloud of these meanings shower rain upon you, that you may drink its blessings.

Know, may the Lord have mercy on you and guide you to the station of the blessed contact, that sitting knee-to-knee is the

1 Muslim, *Ṣaḥīḥ*, K. al-Īmān, 8. Trans. Murata and Chittick, with some modifications.

meaning of contact between the realities of prophethood and messengerhood in the nearness of sainthood. This is the station of companionship and brotherhood, wherein the Beloved ﷺ was in the station of prophethood while Gabriel was in the station of messengerhood. When they sat knee-to-knee, the Alif became manifest, and God's straight path was disclosed in the material realm.

One must therefore halt with the words, in the hope of catching the scent of their spirit. Reflect, may God have mercy on you, on al-Fārūq's taste when he said, "he sat down with the Prophet." He did not say "with the Messenger," for Gabriel himself had come in the role of messenger, and the prophetic half of the Alif remained disclosed in the form of the Beloved ﷺ. The Alif was therefore completed by the meeting of the Messenger Gabriel and the Prophet Muḥammad ﷺ. As for how Gabriel came in the form of a man, it was because he had come to the Muḥammadan form in the prophetic mosque, ennobled by God. If he had descended to a star, he would have taken on his form as it is in the spiritual world.

Contact, then, is the meeting-point of the realities that flow in the disclosure-site of the World of Invincibility, through which are birthed other infinite realities. One of its forms is the pledge of allegiance between Shaykh and disciple. The pledge involves contact between the hands of the Shaykh and disciple: **Truly those who pledge allegiance unto thee pledge allegiance only unto God. The Hand of God is over their hands. And whosoever reneges, reneges only to his detri-**

ment. And whosoever fulfills what He has pledged unto God, He will grant him a great reward.[1] Hand-to-hand contact prompts the descent of the realities of the pledge of attribute; head-to-head contact prompts the descent of the realities of the pledge of vicegerency. Each contact provides a different reality from the other.

If you are astute, you will derive from this hadith the proper courtesy to maintain when in the presence of your Shaykh. Even if you have mastered the station of sainthood's messengerhood and the secret of transmission, as long as you are in the presence of your Mediator you must descend to the station of sainthood's prophethood—unless your Shaykh gives you permission, whereupon you may speak with the voice of his messengerhood and the aspiration of his prophethood, so that he is the one speaking through you, just as God was the One Who threw when the Prophet threw: **thou threwest not when thou threwest, but God threw.**[2]

1 Q Fatḥ 48:10.
2 Q Anfāl 8:17.

Exclusive Singularity (*tafrīd*)

Know, may God watch over you, that exclusive singularity is a unique science and a sublime secret in the hearts of the people of the everlasting presence and the core of the Alif of existence. The one who declares God's unity is not like the one who upholds His exclusive singularity; in fact, there is a vast difference between the two, though there is goodness in both.

Our science is based upon the majestic word, *Allāh*. Through it all beings subsist. If its people were to vanish, existence itself would cease, and the world would come to ruin. An authentic hadith says, "The Hour will not rise until *Allāh, Allāh* is no longer uttered upon the earth."[1] The secret of the veneration of the Name by the Sufi masters is that it does not depart from the Named. It is not like the names of created things; for when you utter the name of a created thing, the thing might be absent. You might say "Zayd" when Zayd is not around. But when you say *Allāh*, He is present with you.

1 Muslim, *Ṣaḥīḥ*, K. al-Īmān, #148a.

What, then, is the difference between God's unity (*tawḥīd*) and His exclusive singularity (*tafrīd*)?

Know that unity implies the prior existence of multiplicity; it means to return from separation to union, to gather the parts of the cosmic form unto one ultimate form. If you say "the community has been united," you mean that it has come to follow a single path after having previously been dispersed among differing paths. When a person unites his thoughts, he summons his divergent thoughts into a single thought. Likewise—and God is beyond compare—the science of divine unity is to collect many meanings into a single secret, to behold the objects of witnessing through the glass of union. Its station is the station of *Lillāh*, "to God."

What, then, is the station of *Lillāh*?

It is the Hā' of Identity, the Lām of Love, and the Lām of Gnosis.

In the Hā' of Identity, you united existence within the manifestation-sites of the existent, and came to know that there is no existent but the Lord. You understood that **All that is upon it passes away, and there remains the Face of thy Lord, Possessed of Majesty and Bounty,**[1] and that "The truest word a poet ever uttered was what Labīd said: 'Truly, everything apart from God is unreal, and every delight must come to an end.'"[2]

1 Q Raḥmān 55:26-27.
2 Muslim, *Ṣaḥīḥ*, K. al-Shi'r, #2256.

Then in the Lām of Love, you melted in the ocean of the Mediator, and united the spirit of the Yearned-For with the atoms of existence. You came to know that **Unto Him belongs sovereignty over the heavens and the earth,**[1] and that every drop in the ocean of existence proceeds from Him, guides to Him, and points to Him through the allusion of **there is no god but You.**[2]

Then in the Lām of Gnosis, you bore witness to the unity of the yearner and the Yearned-For; and in the sacred valley of the knowledge of Ṭuwā, you removed the shoes of "I" and caprice, and became like Laylā's Majnūn, singing, "I am Laylā!" Nothing remains in you but the meaning of the allusion of **Truly I am God, there is no god but I. So worship Me, and perform the prayer for the remembrance of Me.**[3]

Then you entered into the enclosed ocean of separation, where complete incineration takes place. The measured-out ordinances of arrival at the everlasting presence begin to manifest to you, where there is contact with the liminality of sainthood and the wellspring of exclusive singularity.

The Hidden Alif is thus where exclusive singularity begins, because you are no longer pursuing unity, for you no longer have any "prior", nor any "other", nor any "besides." You have become the manifestation-site of unity yourself, and exclusive singularity has become your goal.

1 Q Ḥadīd 57:2.
2 Q Anbiyāʾ 21:87.
3 Q Ṭā Hā 20:14.

This is the difference between unity and exclusive singularity. Some masters have called it "the oneness of the all and the allness of oneness" (*aḥadiyyat al-jumūʿ wa-majmūʿ al-aḥadiyya*). Divine unity is the oneness of the all; the search for the identity of the Essence in every disclosure, every manifestation, and every perspective, whether it be a name or an attribute of these worlds.

As for the allness of oneness, it is the Hidden Alif where lies sheer singularity and the universal all, which gives forth only the holiest meaning and is transcendent beyond every perspective.

At Last, ʿUmar!

ʿAbd Allāh b. Hishām related that the Prophet ﷺ was once holding the hand of ʿUmar b. al-Khaṭṭāb when ʿUmar said: "Messenger of God, you are more beloved unto me than everything except my own soul." The Prophet ﷺ said, "Nay, by the One in Whose Hand is my soul, not until I am more beloved to you than yourself." ʿUmar said, "Now, by God, you are indeed more beloved unto me than myself." The Prophet ﷺ said, "At last, ʿUmar!"[1]

Know, dear wayfarer, that none will find success on the path but those who are honest with themselves, with their Shaykh, and with their Lord. Look at how truthful al-Fārūq was, how he told the Prophet ﷺ exactly what was in his heart and swore it by God. No liar may set foot in the everlasting station; for just as it is impossible for the Prophets to tell lies, lying does not befit the wayfarers in this sublime station. You must strive for sincerity in your speech and action, until you are written down as a person of truthfulness (*ṣiddīq*). A tradition says, "A man goes on telling the truth, and striving for truthfulness, until he is written down as a man of truthfulness. Another man goes on telling lies, and striving for falsehood, until he is written down

1 Bukhārī, *Ṣaḥīḥ*, K. al-Īmān wa'l-Nudhūr, #6257.

with God as a liar."[1] The narration of Bukhārī and Muslim has, "You must be truthful, for truthfulness leads to righteousness, and righteousness leads to Paradise. A man goes on telling the truth, and striving for truthfulness, until he is written down with God as a man of truthfulness. Beware of lying, for lying leads to iniquity, and iniquity leads to Hell. A man goes on telling lies, and striving for falsehood, until he is written down with God as a liar."[2]

Note also how the Prophet ﷺ required of ʿUmar that he be more beloved to him than his own self. Another hadith says, "None of you has faith until I am more beloved to him than his child, his father, and all people."[3] Notice that he did not require that they love him more than they loved themselves in order to have faith, but he did require this of ʿUmar. This is because ʿUmar had a special station, the station of inheritance in the disclosure-site of prophethood. Another hadith from the Chosen Prophet ﷺ states this explicitly: "In the communities before you, there were people who were inspired [*muḥaddathūn*]. If there is one in my community, it is ʿUmar."[4] Ibn ʿAbbās used to recite the verse, **And no messenger or prophet did We send before thee...**,[5] adding "**or inspired one**" after "**or prophet**." The reason ʿUmar was singled out for mention here was because of the many occasions during the time of the Prophet ﷺ when

1 Aḥmad, *Musnad*, #4044.
2 Muslim, *Ṣaḥīḥ*, K. al-Birr, #2607.
3 Bukhārī, *Ṣaḥīḥ*, K. al-Īmān, #15.
4 Bukhārī, *Ṣaḥīḥ*, K. Aḥādīth al-Anbiyāʾ, #3469.
5 Q Ḥajj 22:52.

his opinions were confirmed by Qur'ānic revelations.

So in order to enter the station of the inheritance of the prophethood of sainthood, you must be annihilated in your Shaykh and consumed with love for him. Love is not a matter of talk, but of action—yes, action, which you will recognize from yourself. Whenever a wayfarer lays claim to a station, God tests him. If you claim that you love your Mediator and are annihilated in him, prepare to be tested. Only then will you be worthy of this station.

The Light of Your Prophet, O Jābir

It is the Light of the Prophet of God. Yes—it was for him that existence existed, and for him that it came into being. Know, dear wayfarer, that prophethood from him ﷺ is the journey of unseen nonmanifestation from the station of "I loved to be known," and the dialogue of the names in the presence of the Named, until the time of the public proclamation of the message. It is the nonmanifest flow of all those realities. Jābir, may God be pleased with him, saw this in summation in the Light of the Prophet ﷺ; and then the Prophet divulged to him how it was the disclosure-site of "the Light of your Prophet, O Jābir," after acquainting him with it in detail.

Just so, dear wayfarer, you are from the Light of your Prophet in the attribute of sainthood, and you must return with it to pre-existence, so that its pre-eternal magnificence, majesty, and beauty may be manifested to you. There you will behold how it flows through the levels of existence, how it descends in the veils, and how it manifests in the stations. Thus you will grasp the tremendous importance of your Mediator, and recognize how he has been alive for time immemorial; how he was before every before, and will be after every after. Ibn al-Fāriḍ said of this, may God sanctify his spirit:

Remembering the beloved, we drank a wine;
It made us drunk before the creation of the vine.

Sun poured into full moon, passed round by crescent,
How many stars shone forth when it was blended!

He tells of how he became drunk on the love of the presence before grapes were even created, let alone pressed. How could he have become drunk when the intoxicating substance did not yet exist? This is a reality that none grasp but the people of sublime ascension in the presence of "peace be upon us, and upon God's righteous servants."

You will behold the Light of the Mediator in the measure of your station, not his. If your aspiration remains non-differentiated and stitched, you will see him in summation as if he is a star, moon, or sun. But if you float with him in unstitched differentiation, you will see most wondrous things, and learn from him what was and what shall be; for all existence is folded up within him.

This hadith also contains an allusion to those who lay claim to shaykh-hood, the ones who say "my father was so-and-so." Do they have any Light, that they might bring it down into the hearts of their disciples? Will their lamps shine forth with Light kindled from the Blessed Tree, like a Niche, a Lamp, a Glass, or a Resplendent Planet? Can they truthfully claim, "This is the Light of your Shaykh"? The one who does not have the power to do this lacks enough Light even to cross the street! If he has no Light, no initiatic chain, and no gnosis, how can he be a guide? How can the blind lead the blind?

Dear wayfarer, strive and struggle as earnestly as you can, until you come to know the differentiated Light of the Mediator, and through it grasp the spirit of the world and the secret of the prophethood of sainthood.

VII – Messengerhood (*Risāla*)

And know that the Messenger of God is among you.

Messengerhood

Know, dear wayfarer, that in this station you revolve in the orbit of messengerhood, and the most you can be is one of its shadows, that perhaps you may be graced with contact with the intellect of the Chosen Prophet ﷺ. For this is why his name is linked to the name of the Lord, and why his contentment is the Lord's contentment. God says, **Whosoever obeys the Messenger obeys God.**[1]

Know that the intellect (*'aql*) is not like the inner heart (*fu'ād*). The inner heart is the kernel (*lubb*) of the intellect, and God speaks directly to those who have kernels: **Yet none remember save the possessors of kernels.**[2] None remember the primordial covenants in the atomic world except those who possess kernels. He also says: **Truly in the creation of the heavens and the earth and the variation of the night and the day are signs for the possessors of kernels.**[3] Furthermore, they are the only ones who grasp the secrets of the diverse signs of creation, for they are the locus of the divine gaze and the disclosure-site of the secret of eternity, which will be divulged to those for whom God has opened the eye of the heart, those whom He

1 Q Nisā' 4:80.
2 Q Baqara 2:269.
3 Q Āl 'Imrān 3:190.

has graced with submission unto the possessors of kernels. One who receives this grace will belittle his own existence before theirs, and see himself as their servant, an inmate in the prison of their service.

Know also that the intellect is the Tablet. A tradition says, "The first thing God created was the intellect. He said to it, 'Advance', and it advanced. Then He said to it, 'Retreat', and it retreated. Then He said, 'By My might and My majesty, I have not created anything nobler in My sight than you. Through you I take, and through you I give, and through you I reward, and through you I punish.'" The Tablet, the Pen, the Throne, and the Pedestal are disclosure-sites of the intellect. In his sensory composition, the human being has an intellect in every sensation. It was in this intellect that the time of **Yea, we bear witness** was engraved, which is what was written before you. The Pen of divine power wrote it upon the Tablet of your soul, and you cannot stray outside it even a hair's breadth, nor swerve from that for which you were created.

The two *Ṣaḥīḥ* collections contain the saying of the Prophet ﷺ, "Each one of you is assembled in the womb of his mother in forty days, and then becomes a clot for a similar period, and then a morsel of flesh for a similar period. Then God sends to him an angel to breathe the spirit into him. The angel is commanded to record four things in a book: his provision, his life-span, his deeds, and whether he is wretched or felicitous. By God, besides whom there is no other god, one of you may do the deeds of the Paradise-bound till there is only a cubit between him and Paradise, but then the book catches up with him, and he does the deeds of the Hell-bound, and enters Hell. And another of you may do the deeds of the Hell-bound till there is only a cubit between him and Hell, but then the book catches up with him, and he does the deeds of the Paradise-bound, and enters Paradise."[1]

On the level of the disclosure-site of the atom, all are equal, for they all testified against themselves, as God says: **And when thy Lord took from the Children of Adam, from their loins, their seeds and made them bear witness concerning themselves, "Am I not your Lord?" they said, "Yea, we bear witness"— lest you should say on the Day of Resurrection, "Truly of this we were heedless."**[2] This testimony— if we may be permitted to give an example in the language of our era—is akin to an encryption that is encoded into every intellect. The Mediator is the one who is permitted to decipher this encryption. When the encryption of messengerhood is deciphered for someone, the laws of revelation and the secrets of interpretation become manifest to him, and he understands the meaning of the Law and his relationship with the Lawgiver. This is why it is said that the companionship between the Shaykh and the disciples is a companionship of reflection; they are like the stars, and he is like the sun from which they draw, for he is the heir of the secret of the dot under the Bā' of the basmala.

1 Bukhārī, *Ṣaḥīḥ*, K. Aḥādīth al-Anbiyā', #3332.

2 Q A'rāf 7:172.

The heir of the secret of messengerhood is an intellect wherein is gathered the Lights of the stars and all the disclosure-sites of the intellect that are deposited in them. However, it is encrypted and can only be deciphered by beholding the star of Sirius. By beholding it, everything deposited by the preordinance of divine power will become manifest in the heaven of your heart.

The Qurʾān is the intellect of the cosmos. The intellect of the Holy Qurʾān is the Fātiḥa. The intellect of the Fātiḥa is the basmala. The intellect of the basmala is the Bāʾ. The secret of the Bāʾ is the Dot. The Shaykh is the disclosure-site of the Dot in your era, and therefore everything in the cosmos is gathered within him. He kindles himself by himself by way of **God is the Friend.**[1] He has knowledge of the secret of messengerhood and the threads of revelation, which he may weave as he pleases according to the knowledge of divine decree, the secret of predestination, and the disclosure-site of the now.

1 Q Baqara 2:257.

The Messenger's Messenger

Muʿādh, may God be pleased with him, related that when the Prophet ﷺ sent him to Yemen, he said to him, "If you should be required to pass judgment, how will you rule?" He replied, "I will rule by what the Book of God says." He said, "And if it is not in the Book of God?" He replied, "Then by the Sunna of God's Messenger ﷺ." He said, "And if it is not in the Sunna of the Messenger of God?" He replied, "I will exercise my reasoning, and spare no effort." The Messenger of God ﷺ struck his chest and exclaimed, "Praise be to God, who has guided the messenger of God's Messenger to what pleases God's Messenger!"[1]

Know, dear wayfarer, that one way in which the role of Prophet is different from that of Messenger is that a Prophet must be a human being, while a Messenger could be an angel. The Almighty says: **God chooses messengers from among the angels and from among mankind. Truly God is Hearing, Seeing.**[2] One thing prophethood and messengerhood have in common is that neither role is assigned to women. Another is that both the Prophet and the Messenger receive a law by revelation. However, the Messenger's law is new, while the Prophet

1 Abū Dāwūd, *Sunan*, K. al-Aqḍiya, #2592.
2 Q Ḥajj 22:75.

follows the law of the Messenger who preceded him. The Prophet is the one in whom the meaning is inspired, but it is meant especially for him and he is not commanded to preach it to anyone so that they may follow him.

Know also, may God guide you to the path of sincerity, that we are entering the seventh station of the Hāʾ-reading, in order to study the secrets of the upper half of the Hidden Alif, which concerns the presence of messengerhood. This upper half is wrapped in the garment of eternity, swaddled in the mantle of divine protection. The one who occupies it is not at risk of infringement, nor subject to error. His knowledge is from God's knowledge, and he is surrounded by God's nurture, protection, and shelter in every motion and stillness.

The science of messengerhood was transmitted in the form of milk. Its station begins at the Pedestal, for it is the disclosure-site of command and prohibition, which is identical with the station of lawgiving. It is a matter of sheer divine election, not something acquirable. It affirms for God the attribute of speech, for the Messenger conveys what is said to him when he is told, **Say!**. The message is the pre-eternal divine speech with which the Messenger is sent, and commanded to convey by a divine command. This is why we said that messengerhood ceases when the conveyance of the message ceases. The Messenger may receive the message by the mediation of the Holy Spirit, which blows into his soul, as the Prophet ﷺ said: "The Holy Spirit blew into my soul: No soul dies until its provision is completed, so reverence God and seek it by beautiful means.

Do not let your impatience for provision drive you to seek it by disobeying God; for what is with God can only be grasped by obeying Him."[1]

Know also that messengerhood has come to an end, but inspiration without legislation has not ceased. It remains by virtue of the Muḥammadan legacy in the form of the descents of the secrets of the Qur'ān into the hearts of God's righteous servants. This is a spiritual inspiration of the meanings of the Qur'ān. If they are commanded to convey it, they become, like the Messengers, obliged to convey it. But this does not mean that the Law is altered, for the Law remains unchanged, its rulings firm, its commandments and prohibitions free of any addition or subtraction. *The saint does not bring a new law, but only a new understanding.* Remember this principle, for it will protect you from going astray.

Know also that understanding from God and His Messenger is the mark of supreme truthfulness and the banner of sainthood. None is granted it but a servant with a clean heart that has become full of the Light of the Beloved ﷺ, so that he receives the secrets of messengerhood by the Lights of the Messenger ﷺ, not by himself. 'Alī ibn Abī Ṭālib, may God ennoble his countenance, was once asked, "Did the Messenger of God ﷺ single you out for anything, apart from the rest of the people?" He replied, "No, by the One Who split the seed and created mankind, except for an understanding that God may give a

1 Arna'ūṭ, *Takhrīj Zād al-ma'ād*, 1/77; Albānī, *Ṣaḥīḥ al-jāmi'*, #2085.

servant of His Book, and what is written upon this document."[1] The document concerned the rulings on blood indemnities, the freeing of prisoners, and the penalty for a Muslim who murders an unbeliever.

If you desire further clarification, then the Qur'ānic descents can only occur to a heart that is pure and purified, chosen by God to receive spiritual inspiration, as alluded to in His words: **The Raiser of degrees, the Possessor of the Throne, He casts the Spirit from His Command upon whomsoever He will among His servants to warn of the Day of the Meeting.**[2] Know also that the Messengers are bearers of glad tidings and warnings, and the saint can also convey tidings and warnings, but not qualified with rewards and punishments. The Messenger, on the other hand, conveys a glad tiding and qualifies it with a particular reward, which none but a Messenger may do. In a manner of speaking, he offers you a deal, and if you accept it you become one of the saved, while otherwise you do not. Or one might say that he offers glad tidings to the non-believer in the midst of his unbelief, and warns the believer in the midst of his belief, such as in the hadith about the [damnation of the] one who kills himself during jihad. This is specific to the Messenger, and sainthood plays no part in it. However, the saints do retain the attribute of power, and so a saint may tell you, for instance, that a certain person is from the people of goodness, or has goodness in him, or that he has a tremendous future

1 Tirmidhī, *Jāmiʿ*, K. al-Diyāt, #1412.

2 Q Ghāfir 40:15.

ahead of him, without qualifying this with a particular deed. This results from a particular disclosure through which the saints recognize such things. It is from the prophethood of tiding, not the prophethood of lawgiving.

Messengerhood is from the station of the Pedestal, and thus is especially for those whose intellects are vast; for compared to the Pedestal, all the worlds are like a ring thrown down upon open ground. Messengerhood thus begins at the Pedestal and ends at the Lote Tree of the Furthest Boundary. Our master Muḥammad ﷺ entered the Lote Tree by virtue of the station of messengerhood, and returned with the laws concerning canonical prayer. Human messengerhood has many meanings, and comes with the meaning of servanthood, poverty, and non-divinity. This is why the Almighty so often takes pains to affirm their humanity, lest any other ideas be entertained about them. Messengerhood is the furthest boundary of the Perfect Human Being, which is why it has the right to return to the Lote Tree of the Furthest Boundary: "Be Muḥammad!" The Handful of Light descended into a perfect, pure, and purified form, and was Muḥammad ibn 'Abd Allāh by virtue of messengerhood. Then it returned with this form to the Handful by virtue of the sainthood of "peace be upon us, and upon God's righteous servants."

Know also that the Muḥammadan messengerhood of the Chosen Prophet ﷺ is the most perfect disclosure of the Real. For, by virtue of the names, he possesses the disclosure of the all-encompassing name *Allāh*, to the extent that God said of him, **Thou threwest not when thou threwest, but God threw,**[1] and, **Truly those who pledge allegiance unto thee pledge allegiance only unto God. The Hand of God is over their hands.**[2] Thus he possesses the secrets of the all-encompassing name exclusively, while the other Prophets possess the other disclosures of the names. For example, our master Jesus, upon him be peace, possesses the disclosure of the name the All-Powerful, which is why he could raise the dead by God's power.

In this station—the messengerhood of sainthood—you share the role of the Messenger's messenger with Muʿādh; for the Messenger ﷺ made us all vicegerents by saying, "Convey from me, even if only a single verse; and relate the stories of the Israelites, no harm. But he who willfully tells a lie about me may take his seat in Hell."[3] That is a general vicegerency. Moreover, there is a special type of vicegerency in this sublime station, namely when the news that is conveyed is newly arrived from God, such that the words issue from one who is living, from a heart to which the Everlasting Alif has disclosed itself, a heart wherein the sciences of revelation and the secrets of esoteric interpretation have been stored.

1 Q Anfāl 8:17.
2 Q Fatḥ 48:10.
3 Bukhārī, *Ṣaḥīḥ*, K. Aḥādīth al-Anbiyā', #3461.

Conveying the Message (*tablīgh*)

The Beloved ﷺ said, "Let those of you who witness convey to those who are absent."[1]

Know, dear disciple, that according to the people of meaning, the witness is the one who is present in the presence of witnessing to receive the command from him ﷺ firsthand. This witness is commanded to convey, and so becomes the messenger of God's Messenger ﷺ. In a certain sense this means that he is "with" the Master of Messengerhood, as God says, **Muhammad is the Messenger of God. Those who are with him...**[2] Those who are with him are those who have permission to convey the message because of what they have witnessed firsthand from his blessed presence.

Now since God sent His Messenger our master Muḥammad ﷺ **as a mercy to the worlds,**[3] his message must be a mercy to all people, for He commanded him to convey it, saying, **O Messenger! Convey that which has been sent down unto thee from thy Lord;**[4] **And if they turn away, We sent thee not as a keeper over them. Naught is incumbent upon thee, save the**

1 Bukhārī, *Ṣaḥīḥ*, K. al-ʿIlm, #103.

2 Q Fatḥ 48:29.

3 Q Anbiyāʾ 21:107.

4 Q Māʾida 5:67.

proclamation;[1] **Thou art not tasked with their guidance, but God guides whomsoever He will.**[2] This means that he is tasked to convey as part of the role of messengerhood, but he is not tasked to guide, for that is for God alone. God says: **Surely thou dost not guide whomsoever thou lovest, but God guides whomsoever He will.**[3] God is the Guide by virtue of the name *al-Walī*, the Friend, for he brings people out of the compound darkness of ignorance and error into the Light of knowledge and guidance. God says, **God is the Friend of those who believe. He brings them out of the darkness into the Light.**[4]

Thus, the principle of conveying from the Messenger ﷺ continues to flow through this Community, and will do so until his message covers **all the worlds.** The Prophet ﷺ reportedly said, "May God make radiant the one who hears a saying from us and remembers it until he conveys it to another with a better memory than him, who conveys it to another who understands it better than him. Many a man conveys knowledge he does not understand."[5] This means that one does not truly convey from the presence of messengerhood unless one conveys word-for-word without any alteration, substitution, addition, or subtraction. One conveys what one hears or sees from the Messenger ﷺ exactly as it is. Another narration of the aforementioned hadith on the authority of Ibn Masʿūd, may God be pleased

1 Q Shūrā 42:48.
2 Q Baqara 2:272.
3 Q Qaṣaṣ 28:56.
4 Q Baqara 2:257.
5 Tirmidhī, *Jāmiʿ*, K. al-ʿIlm, #2656.

with him, relates that God's Messenger ﷺ said, "May God make radiant the one who hears something from us and conveys it just as he heard it; for the one to whom something is conveyed may understand it better than the one who heard it."[1] This excludes the one who merely conveys what he understands from the Chosen Prophet ﷺ, for such a person is really only conveying from himself. The attempt to understand a source is one thing, and the source itself is another.

Conveying the message, then, is for the people of the messengerhood of sainthood in our time, those to whom the Lord has permitted the secret of the Alif of Divine Measuring. They are the ones who have the authority of sending-down and the understanding of the divine laws. By the secret of the Alif, they know the measures of guidance that best suit their times, and bring down the messages of sublime glorifications in the forms of acts of worship, invocations, and devotions. For example, the phrase *subḥān Allāh*, "God be glorified," is a palm tree in Paradise, but when you utter it in the sensory world with the tongue of invocation, it is as if you are planting a palm tree in the unseen world. What is the relationship between *subḥān Allāh* and the palm tree in Paradise? That is the secret of the those who are worthy of conveying.

In order to become among those who are worthy of conveying, you must first be among those who weave the threads of divine measuring between the unseen world and the visible

1 Nawawī, *Riyāḍ al-ṣāliḥīn*, #1389.

world, so that you come to know what delimited intellects are capable of and what they are not, and what corporeal beings are able to bear and what they are not, and what is suitable for some moments but not others.

These are among the arts of shaykh-hood, the arts of the lordly servants who mentor their pupils in minor matters before major ones. They show the disciple in each moment what suits him with regards to his worldly life and his hereafter, so that he attains peace in this life and Paradise in the next through the blessing of their direction. Anyone who allows his soul to convince him to contravene their guidance will find himself hurled to and fro by caprice through halls of darkness, and things will present themselves to him in illusory forms, for they have no basis in the reality of divine measuring. He will continue to worship a mirage bereft of the water of recompense; and when he comes to it on the Day of Resurrection, he will find that it is nothing: **As for those who disbelieve, their deeds are like a mirage upon a desert plain which a thirsty man supposes is water, till when he comes upon it, he does not find it to be anything, but finds God there. He will then pay him his reckoning in full, and God is swift in reckoning.**[1]

1 Q Nūr 24:39.

The Sending-Down (*tanzīl*)

Know that disclosure is not attained by thought, but comes from the presence of God from His Name *al-Qahhār*, the All-Subjugating. You must understand the message for whose sake He showed you the disclosure. Disclosures are silent texts, just as the cosmos is a silent Qur'ān. You must decode their meanings into experiential knowledge. An example of this is the interpretation of milk to mean knowledge; that is, knowledge is a meaning that is disclosed in the form of milk. 'Abd Allāh b. 'Umar related that he heard God's Messenger ﷺ say, "As I was sleeping, I was brought a cup of milk. I drank from it until I could see the liquid emerging from my fingertips. Then what was left over was given to you," meaning 'Umar. The people said, "How do you interpret it, Messenger of God?" He replied, "Knowledge."[1]

When the disciple is sitting invoking his Lord and holy disclosures come to him, these disclosures are levels and meanings delimited in forms so that they are easier to comprehend. Seeing them is like learning the title of the book. If he desires the meaning, he must grasp what lies beyond the form. In this regard, reflect on the story of Moses, upon him be peace, and

1 Bukhārī, *Ṣaḥīḥ*, K. al-Ta'bīr, #7006.

the beatific vision. After hearing the words, **Thou shalt not see Me**, he was told, **look upon the mountain**; that is, **look upon** the form; for when someone halts with the form of the disclosure, it is a genuine vision. But our master Moses desired the meaning and the source: **And when his Lord manifested Himself to the mountain, He made it crumble to dust, and Moses fell down in a swoon.**[1] When he became annihilated and swooned, he recognized the meaning and the secret, and returned to the form of the disclosure, and then asked forgiveness and repented. From this Mosaic waystation, the disciple follows the footsteps of prophethood and messengerhood, because God appointed the Prophets as exemplars to be followed both outwardly and inwardly. Therefore, when the disciple halts with the form of the disclosure, he attains the title of knowledge; and when he grasps what lies behind the form, he reaches knowledge itself. When you are with the forms of disclosure, it is as if Mount Ṭūr has manifested to you, while its crumbling is veiled from you. You must cast the Light of faith upon the form of the disclosure until it crumbles and disappears from your view. Only then will you recognize the secrets and sciences that lie beyond it. This is how wayfaring takes place.

The primal Light of faith is received in the very beginning at the pledge of allegiance. In order to make our meaning clearer to you, let us give you another example. The Prophet ﷺ would

1 Q Aʿrāf 7:143.

never look upon the form of Gabriel when the Qur'ān was sent down, but would look beyond it. The goal was not Gabriel, but the Qur'ān. That is the greater goal, dear disciple, not the form of the disclosure.

Moreover, this is the purpose of messengerhood, namely that you grasp the meaning of its legislations. Acts of worship are conditional upon the revelation, and when it comes to the things the Beloved ﷺ made clear such as prayer, fasting, pilgrimage, and so on, no personal reasoning may be exercised in them. However, everything the Messenger ﷺ brought down has its fruits, just as contravening them has its penalties. One of the secrets of the descents of messengerhood is found in his ﷺ words, "If someone says *subḥān Allāh*, God be glorified, after every prayer thirty-three times, and *Allāhu akbar* (God is great) thirty-three times, and *al-ḥamdu li'Llāh* (God be praised) thirty-three times, and finishes the hundred with, *lā ilāha illā Allāh, waḥdahū lā sharīka lah, lahū l-mulk, wa lahū l-ḥamd, wa-huwa 'alā kulli shay'in qadīr* (there is no god but God, alone without partner; His is the kingdom, and His is the praise, and He is powerful over all things) God will forgive him for all he has done, even if his sins are like the foam of the sea."[1]

Why did the Beloved ﷺ liken sins to the foam of the sea? God says, **Nor does he speak out of caprice. It is naught but a revelation revealed.**[2] Every word the Chosen Prophet ﷺ uttered has its meaning. Indeed, I say that every hadith of the Prophet ﷺ

1 Muslim, *Ṣaḥīḥ*, K. al-Masājid, #597.

2 Q Najm 53:3-4.

has seventy interpretations, corresponding to the number of veils between God and creation.

You know that a hand contains fourteen joints, corresponding to the luminous letters by which God swears an oath. Add the joints of the other hand, the shadows of this luminosity, and you have twenty-eight joints. Then add the moving joint with which you count your glorifications, which is the voweled Hamza, and you have twenty-nine. This is the cycle of the moon, whose Light grows until halfway through the month and then begins to diminish gradually.

You know that the moon influences the tides of the sea and makes it come in and go out, which causes foam to form on it. You also know that you are a copy of mother earth, and that the blood in you is like the sea in her, while your flesh is like her dry land. So when you count the glorifications with your joints, the lunar cycle moves with you in the measure of your aspiration and power. The sea moves with your lunar cycle, and so your sins are forgiven even if they are as numerous as the foam of the sea.

I gave you this example so that you may know that messengerhood is the science of how meaning is sent down to the sensory world, so that the delimited human intellect may receive it in the form of sensory illusions, and understand it—no, be convinced by it—and assume it as a way of life and a religious vocation, and persist in it as worship.

The Fifty and the Five

Anas b. Mālik said:

Abū Dharr used to relate that God's Messenger ﷺ said: "The roof of my house was opened up while I was in Mecca, and Gabriel came down. He opened my breast and then washed it with Zamzam water. Then he brought a golden basin filled with wisdom and faith, and poured it into my breast and then closed it. Then he took my hand and took me up to the lowest heaven. When I reached it, Gabriel told the keeper of Heaven, 'Open!' He said, 'Who is this?' He replied, 'This is Gabriel.' He said, 'Is anyone with you?' He replied, 'Yes, Muḥammad ﷺ is with me.' He said, 'Has he been summoned?' He said, 'Yes.' When he opened, we ascended beyond the lowest heaven and we came across a man sitting there, with a throng to his right and a throng to his left. When he looked to his right he would smile, and when he looked to his left he would weep. He said, 'Welcome, righteous Prophet and righteous son.' I asked Gabriel, 'Who is this?' He said, 'This is Adam, and these throngs to his right and his left are the spirits of his progeny. Those on the right are the people of Paradise, and the throng on his left are the people of Hell. When he looks to his right he smiles, and when he looks to his left he weeps.'

"Then he took me up to the second heaven and said to its keeper, 'Open.' Its keeper said to him what the first had said, and then opened.'"

Anas said, 'He then told of how while in the heavens he met Adam, Idrīs, Moses, Jesus and Abraham, may God's blessings be upon them all. He did not specify all their positions, apart from saying that he met Adam in the lowest heaven and Abraham in the sixth heaven.' Then Anas said:

When Gabriel took the Prophet ﷺ past Idrīs, he said [the Prophet ﷺ continued]: "Welcome, righteous Prophet and righteous brother.' I said, 'Who is this?' He replied, 'This is Idrīs.' Then I passed by Moses, who said, 'Welcome, righteous Prophet and righteous brother.' I said, 'Who is this?' He replied, 'This is Moses.' Then I passed by Jesus, who said, 'Welcome, righteous brother and righteous Prophet.' I said, 'Who is this?' He replied, 'This is Jesus.' Then I passed by Abraham, who said, 'Welcome, the righteous Prophet and righteous son.' I said, 'Who is this?' He replied, 'This is Abraham ﷺ.'"

Ibn Shihāb reported that Ibn Ḥazm told him that Ibn ʿAbbās and Abū Ḥabba al-Anṣārī used to say that the Prophet ﷺ said, "Then he took me up until I arrived at a level where I could hear the scratching of the pens."

Ibn Ḥazm and Anas b. Mālik related that the Prophet ﷺ said, "Then God prescribed fifty prayers for my Community, and I returned with that, until I passed by Moses and he said, 'What has God prescribed for your Community?' I replied, 'He prescribed fifty prayers.' He said, 'Return to your Lord, for your

Community will not be able to do that.' He addressed me once more, and reduced them by half. I returned to Moses and said, 'He reduced them by half.' He said, 'Address your Lord once more, for your Community will not be able to do that.' I addressed Him once more, and He reduced them by half. I returned to Moses and said, 'He has reduced them by half.' He said, 'Return to your Lord, for your community will not be able to do that.' I addressed Him once more, and He said, 'They are five, and they are fifty. My Word does not change.' I returned to Moses, and he said 'Address your Lord once more;' but I replied, 'I am shy of my Lord.'

"Then he took me up to the Lote Tree of the Furthest Boundary, which was covered with colors that were unknown to me. Then I was admitted into Paradise, and in it were strings of pearls and its earth was musk."[1]

The Community attained all of this goodness by the blessing of the Supreme Messenger, our master Muḥammad ﷺ. It was all down to his singular weaving, which put the world of illusion in an order so perfect that no one could describe it. He brought a law that applies to all times, moments, states, and communities; and were it not for his weaving, we would not have this blessing. This is why messengerhood was sealed by him, so that his law will never be superseded, nor will his prophethood ever be out of date. All are subject to his command; all revolve in his orbit.

1 Bukhārī, *Ṣaḥīḥ*, K. al-Ṣalāh, #349.

By the secret of this unswerving law, it is decreed that for us, the Community Shown Mercy, repentance is a matter of renouncing sin in private. As for the Israelites, their sins would appear written upon the doors of their houses. And because of the merit of this Muḥammadan Community, Moses the Confidant of God asked to be counted among the community of the Chosen Prophet ﷺ.

Ibn Abī ʿĀṣim narrates in *Kitāb al-Sunna* on the authority of Anas that God's Messenger ﷺ said,

"Moses son of ʿImrān ﷺ was walking down the road one day when the Almighty called to him, 'Moses!' He looked right and left, but saw no one. Then He called him a second time, 'Moses son of ʿImrān!' He looked right and left, but saw no one, and became stricken with fear. Then He called him a third time, 'Moses son of ʿImrān! I am God! There is no god but Me.' He replied, 'At Your service,' and fell down in prostration to God. He said, 'Lift your head, Moses son of ʿImrān.' He lifted his head. God said, 'Moses, do you wish to reside in the shade of My Throne on the day when there is no shade but Mine? Moses, then be like a merciful father to the orphan, and a loving husband to the widow. Moses, show mercy, and you will be shown mercy. Moses, as you judge so shall you be judged. Moses, Prophet of the Israelites! Anyone who meets me and denies Muḥammad, I shall send him to Hell, even if he be My Intimate Abraham, or My Confidant Moses.' He said, 'My God, who is Aḥmad?' He replied, 'Moses, by My might and My majesty, I have created nothing more beloved to Me than him. I wrote his name with Mine upon the Throne two thousand thousand years before I created the heavens, the earth, the sun, and the moon. By My might and My majesty, Paradise will be forbidden to all My creatures until Muḥammad and his Community enter it.'

"Moses said, 'Who are the Community of Muḥammad?' He replied, 'His Community are the praise-givers (*al-ḥammādūn*). They praise when they rise, and when they fall, and in every state. They tie their middles, and purify their extremities. They fast by day, and keep vigil by night. Yet even a little will I accept from them, for I will admit them into Paradise for testifying that there is no god but God.'

"Moses said, 'My God, make me the Prophet of that Community!' He replied, 'Their Prophet shall be one of them.' He said, 'Then make me one of that Prophet's Community!' He replied, 'Your time is now, Moses, and theirs will not be till later. But I will bring you together with him in the Abode of Majesty.'"[1]

1 Ibn Abī 'Āṣim, *al-Sunna*, Bāb Nisbat al-Rabb, #696.

Witnessing the Periphery, and the Periphery of Witnessing

Dear wayfarer, may the Lord guide you to sound understanding—know that the secret of messengerhood begets witnessing of the periphery (*iḥāṭa*) around the central point of descending revelations (*markaz al-tanzīl*). For the role of messengerhood in existence is to send down meanings into the receptacles of physical beings according to the wisdom of the divine pre-ordinance, and in a manner that the vessels of divine decree can contain in the moment. Since the actions of divine law are manifested openly on the human body, the one through whom they are sent down is the focal point of the periphery. To some of them God has granted self-surrender and reverence, so that the form does not veil them from the station. Others do not look to the form to begin with; they are people of annihilation in the Beloved, may God make us among them.

Then there are some who are deceived by the human nature of the one through whom the revelation is sent down, as God says: **And they say, "What ails this Messenger, who eats food and walks in the markets? Why is there not an angel sent down unto him to be a warner with him, or no treasure cast unto him, or no garden for him from which to eat?" And the**

wrongdoers say, "You follow naught but a man bewitched."[1] Others are deceived by his deeds when they differ from the customs of their forefathers and ancestors, as God says: **When it is said unto them, "Follow what God has sent down," they say, "Nay, we follow that which we found our fathers doing." What! Even though their fathers understood nothing, and were not rightly guided?**[2] So when the science of the now is sent down through the Mediator and differs with what they have read in books about the unswerving Sacred Law, they rant and rave and turn upon their heels. This is the condition of most of those who do not understand the secrets of the Sacred Law, but only halt with the outward teachings of the canonical schools. They do not comprehend, but only blindly follow without any understanding of the purposes of the Law.

God says: **How will it be when We bring forth a witness from every community, and We bring thee as a witness against these?**[3] When the Chosen Prophet ﷺ recited this verse, his eyes would well with tears on account of the secrets he knew. He would only ever want his testimony to be for us, not against us. In his prophethood, he is a witness against us; in his messengerhood, his community themselves bear witness to the Law that was sent down through him in the form of his words, deeds, approvals, and states. Thus God follows the aforementioned verse by saying: **On that Day those who disbelieved and**

1 Q Furqān 25:7-8.
2 Q Baqara 2:170.
3 Q Nisāʾ 4:41.

disobeyed the Messenger will wish that they were level with the earth, and they will conceal no account from God.[1] They only disobeyed him because they witnessed the deed and falsified it by not following it.

This is the difference between the secret of prophethood and the secret of messengerhood. With prophethood, you are a witness over your periphery; with messengerhood, your periphery is a witness over you. The science of prophethood allows you to see the unseen things of the spiritual world, such that you are a witness over the periphery in the measure of the affinity between the sensory realm and the realm of pure meaning. As for messengerhood, the act descends to the material world so that the periphery is witness to the acts of worship it beholds as the Messenger performs them.

This tremendous secret, the secret of messengerhood, is beyond the capacity of all but those who have verified the truth, and those who have authority in the world of the laws that pertain to the Real. Many of the people of unveiling cannot bring down the wonders of the spiritual world that they witness in their solitary vigils. But observe, may God have mercy on you, how the Chosen Prophet brought down the Gabrielic form in the form of a man with bright white clothes and jet-black hair, so that all the Companions were able to behold him.

This is one of the levels of the secret of messengerhood, by which the meaning is brought down to the physical realm in

1 Q Nisāʾ 4:42.

accordance with the laws of divine measuring, the concepts of time, space, and number that the mind can comprehend.

A Man Belonging to One Man

Know, dear disciple, that I present this chapter to you that you may taste the state of one who has truly attained the Hidden Alif and found the isthmus between prophethood and messengerhood, so that he may spin the threads of decree from the distaff of sainthood, and weave the laws by the right of **In the Name of God, the All-Merciful, the Ever-Merciful.**

Know, may God have mercy on you, that God's speech in the disclosure-site of every verse is an ocean without a shore. If all creation from first to last come together to interpret it and know the truth of its reality, they would find no way to do so. For it is the speech of the Real, eternal and beginningless, not the speech of creation. It is concealed by the delimitation of the letter so that human tongues can pronounce it and human minds can comprehend it, for otherwise no tongue could utter it, nor any heart grasp it. How fortunate we are to have this mighty Book, which **falsehood cannot approach from before it or from behind it.**[1]

One thing that occurred to me in this exalted station is His words: **God sets forth a parable: a man in whom quarreling partners share, and a man belonging to one man: are the two**

1 Q Fuṣṣilat 41:42.

equal in likeness? Praise be to God! Nay, but most of them know not.[1] Know, dear disciple, that the one in whom **quarreling partners share** is the one who is pulled this way and that by the realities of [the prophetic] presences, and buffeted to and fro by the waves of meanings. He is scattered in the unity of beholding in nearness, veiled by the Real from the Real. He cannot gather the [prophetic] presences in the Seal [of prophethood], nor achieve realization of the gemstone. He is in a perpetual state of disequilibrium, until he attains realization of exalted character.

As for the second, he is the one who is singularly devoted, who witnesses the Real through the Real, protected by God's pre-eternal care, garbed in the everlasting mantle, helped against himself by himself. He has attained the secret of prophethood and messengerhood, known only to his ilk, while most of creation are ignorant of it and oblivious to it. It is to him that God's words allude: **Praise be to God! Nay, but most of them know not.**[2] All things are from him and to him. He possesses the secret of prophethood, by which the realities and origin of things are known; and he possesses the secret of messengerhood, with which the levels of sending-down are weaved. Peace is from him and to him.

These are the ones who seal the secrets of the majestic Name, for they are the true servants of God, while others are the servants of the All-Merciful who have attained no more than the

1 Q Zumar 29:39.
2 Q Luqmān 31:25.

levels of divine measuring. One of them was Christ, upon him be peace, who said, **Truly I am a servant of God,**[1] and also said, **Peace be upon me.**[2] He invoked peace upon himself through himself, which is why he could raise the dead and heal the blind and the leprous. Likewise, the saints among God's servants raise the dead by the Light of the Lord, and heal the ailments of the heart through the pure meanings they bring down to the material world in the form of Sufi wanderings, invocations, and litanies that contain remedies for the sick and antidotes for the heart.

1 Q Maryam 19:30.
2 Q Maryam 19:31.

The Law and the Lawgiver

Know, dear wayfarer, that people devote themselves to the Law like worshippers, and worship the Law through the Law. They are so obsessed with the Path that they forget the Lord of the Path, and overlook how the Law is but a means and not an end. They debate one another's opinions regarding it, which may be all good and well, but the masses go to such ugly extremes in their debates that they forget the higher purpose. You might see one of them pursuing extremely difficult and complicated issues relating to prayer, yet he forgets that prayer is Light, and that its purpose is to be a link between servant and Lord, and that it is the Lord who decides whether it is accepted or not.

Messengerhood in the station of the Hidden Alif is the Path from the Law to the Lawgiver. It is the secret by which the forms of the spiritual world are translated into the deeds of the physical world. But with respect to sainthood, the intention is not to seek the maidens and palaces of Paradise, but to seek the Face of the Forgiving Lord. Sainthood begins at the station of "to worship God as if you see Him," and always circles around the sublime Essence. Paradise, conversely, is a creation, and its bliss too is a creation. God says, **And those who reverence their Lord will be driven to the Garden in throngs, till when they**

reach it, its gates will be opened and its keepers will say unto them, "Peace be upon you; you have done well; so enter it, to abide."[1] The Prophet ﷺ reportedly said, "God is amused by people who will enter Paradise in chains." Another narration has, "who will be dragged into Paradise in chains."[2] They will enter clapped in irons, for they desire only the Face of God. Thus it is said that if the gnostic were never heedless, he would not enter Paradise.[3]

Messengerhood came to show us the path by which we may ascend to understand and know the Lawgiver. Through it, we recognize the blessings of His disclosures from moment to moment, and learn how to interact with them. A tradition says, "Seek goodness at all times, and expose yourselves to God's spiritual breezes; for God has spiritual breezes of His mercy which He sends upon whomever of His servants He will. Ask Him to cover your blemishes, and make tranquil your hearts."[4] Messengerhood directs servants to the acts of worship that draw them nearest God, along with the moments of great blessing that will make the servant's worship acceptable even if his aspiration is weak, because the date, time, and occasion of the worship is particularly apt. These are such times as the month

1 Q Zumar 39:74.

2 Bukhārī, *Ṣaḥīḥ*, K. al-Jihād, #3010.

3 Translator's note: In other words, the gnostic on Judgment Day does not desire to enter the Garden, but rather desires God. In turn, God may cause him to be overcome by heedlessness so that he may be dragged into the Garden in chains. With thanks to Sidi Amine Ghazi.

4 Bayhaqī, *Shu'ab al-Īmān*, Bāb al-Rajā' min al-īmān, #1083.

of Ramaḍān, the days of 'Arafa and 'Āshūrā'; supplicating during travel, at the moment of breaking the fast, or after the canonical prayers; and other such opportunities for drawing closer to God to which the unswerving Sacred Law guides us.

In sum, the Law is but the path to the Lord, and messengerhood came with one side towards the Law and the other towards the presence of the Lawgiver. This has three parts: submission (*islām*), faith (*īmān*), and spiritual excellence (*iḥsān*). Here we are speaking about the station of spiritual excellence in the disclosure-site of the Hidden Alif. We deem the secret of messengerhood to be the secret of the sending-down of meanings into the receptacles of the sensory world, so that they may constitute doors opening into the spiritual world. Messengerhood is like a door with three keys. If you open it with the key of submission, you will find reward and recompense. If you open it with the key of faith, you will find the Lights and wonders of the spiritual world. If you open it with the key of spiritual excellence, you will find God.

Know that the Messenger of God is Among You

God says, **And know that the Messenger of God is among you. Were he to obey you in many matters, you would suffer. But God has caused you to love faith and has made it seem fair in your hearts, and He has caused you to despise disbelief, iniquity, and disobedience—such are the rightly guided.**[1]

The **rightly guided** are those for whom God makes **faith beloved** and **fair in their hearts** by unveiling to them the levels of secrets, until they reach the everlasting presence and see how the connection of messengerhood flows in them. From it they are replenished, and from it they call down the graces that suit each moment. May God have mercy on Mūlāy ʿAbd al-Raḥmān al-Majdhūb (d. 1569), who said,

The day rises over the moon,
And naught but my Lord remains.

The people visit Muḥammad;
As for me, he lives in my heart.

1 Q Ḥujurāt 49:7.

Abū Hurayra related that God's Messenger ﷺ said, "Do not envy one another; do not make false bids; do not harbor anger towards one another; do not alienate one another; do not undercut one another. Be servants of God, brothers. A Muslim is his fellow Muslim's brother. He does not wrong him, betray him, or despise him. Godfearing is here," and he pointed to his chest three times. "It is sufficient evil for a man that he despise his Muslim brother. Every Muslim is inviolable to every other in his blood, his property, and his honor."[1]

The Messenger pointed to his chest because godfearing is in the heart. His Light, which flows in us, is the reality of godfearing, which manifests only to those whom God guides and shows the reality of their own souls. They come to know that the measure of messengerhood in them is by virtue of the Hidden Alif, and so they revere all creation and respect their fellow Muslims because of the Light of primordial disposition that flows in them. Thus the Chosen Prophet said, "It is sufficient evil for a man that he despise his Muslim brother."

Know, furthermore, that the one who attains the secret of messengerhood in the Hidden Alif attains supreme guidance and security from the torment of farness. God says, **God will not punish them while thou art among them.**[2] He is in the everlasting presence with the Prophets and Messengers; **and what beautiful companions they are!**[3]

1 Muslim, *Ṣaḥīḥ*, K. al-Birr, #2564.

2 Q Anfāl 8:33.

3 Q Nisā' 4:69.

The secret of messengerhood, dear wayfarer, is that the Lord has made it a measure for the people of love and self-surrender, but delimited it with the disclosure-site of knowledge by saying, **And know.**[1] It is therefore a secret that must be learned from God's folk, the Shaykhs, the heirs of the Muḥammadan station.

1 Q Ḥujurāt 49:7.

The Muḥammadan Reality (*ḥaqīqa Muḥammadiyya*)

Know, dear seeker of union and wayfarer upon the path of perfection, that we have reached the final allusion in the Book of Messengerhood, regarding the disclosure-site of the Hidden Alif. And what greater way to end than with the Muḥammadan Reality?

Know that this reality is the mercy that encompasses all things, as God says, **My Mercy encompasses all things.**[1] It is through it that mercy is shown to existent beings, for they draw replenishment from it, and are manifested in accordance with its prototypal reality. All existents are shown mercy through it, for mercy precedes wrath, and existence has preponderance over nonexistence.

Know, furthermore, that because God loved to be known, He made the receptacles of existence such that they cannot grasp the meaning of connection or the secret of divine measuring (*taqdīr*) until they ascend to the All-Powerful Measurer (*al-Qadīr*). It is from this love that He created a Beloved, and from it brought the world into existence. He is the connection between eternity and temporality, between servant and Lord, and there-

1 Q Aʿrāf 7:156.

fore is the Fātiḥa of existence. The world is a branch of his reality; he is the Mediator through whose mediation all things in existence were connected to their Creator before they came into manifestation and being.

This is why his name is joined with the Majestic Name, for he is the door. He is the primal Messenger to creation, while all others are his deputies. God says, **And [remember] when God made the covenant of the prophets: "By that which I have given you of a Book and Wisdom, should a messenger then come to you confirming that which is with you, you shall surely believe in him and you shall help him." He said, "Do you agree and take on My burden on these conditions?" They said, "We agree." He said, "Bear witness, for I am with you among those who bear witness."**[1] He did not require the definite article of the Alif and Lām to identify the **messenger**, for that which is already identified does not need defining. God bore witness that he is the master-servant and the cream of existence, may God bless him and give him peace.

Know, dear wayfarer, that we could speak about the Muḥammadan Reality until the ocean of ink ran dry, without giving it its rightful due. However, what you must learn in this station is the reality of reverence to the Mediator through the door of the Muḥammadan Reality which is disclosed in it. You must learn how to become acceptable to it as a disciple, and how to draw nearer to it. It is sufficient pride and honor for you in this

1 Q Āl ʿImrān 3:81.

world that it has unveiled its name to you in the present moment, and brought you near it in the spiritual world. If you are to become worthy of this honor, dear wayfarer, you must devote yourself to its service and to calling unto it, striving for it, and becoming totally annihilated in it with your soul and all your belongings.

Fortunate is the one who makes a bargain with God. What a profitable transaction! **So rejoice in the bargain you have made. That indeed is the great triumph.**[1]

Dear God, by the right of the Light of Your Face, which illuminates all that is dark and sets right the affairs of this world and the next, we ask You to invoke a prayer that is absolute, boundless, and infinite upon the Interpreter of Beginninglessness and the Voice of Endlessness, our master Muḥammad, the Prophet, the one whom You made the all-comprehensive Qurʾān of Your Essence, and the differentiated Furqān of Your attributes. All realities are enveloped in the shade of his reality; all secrets are encased in the shell of his structure.

He is the kingpin of the spirits that roam in the tremendous realm of the Essence, steeped in the bliss of Its absolute beauty that flows in the world of engendered being. He is the one who attests to himself with his words, "He who sees me has seen God," and is attested to by God in His words, **Truly those who pledge allegiance unto thee pledge allegiance only unto God.** He is the one adorned with the Majestic Name, and is **of a tre-**

1 Q Tawba 9:111.

mendous character. He is the veridical mirror; all who look into it recognize themselves; all who plunge into it comprehend its secret; and all who realize it become one with it.

Dear God, give us realization of his reality in every fiber of our beings, so that his absolute beauty may reflect in our delimited bodies, that we may see with his sight, hear with his hearing, grasp with his hand, and walk with his feet. Let his Light purify us from the dross of our souls' darkness. O Most Merciful of the Merciful!

Conclusion

Here ends our discourse on the secrets of divine Identity, and the curtains that the disciple's soul places upon the door of his intellect, veiling him from understanding and confusing the levels for him. His soul does this only because it is certain that if he were to understand the secrets, his understanding would spell the soul's annihilation. Thus, he clasps the secrets in the iron of the Law and imprisons them in the courtyard of independent reasoning.

If God wills, we shall move on to the disclosure-site of the Lām of Passionate Love, until we become totally contracted in the presence of the Beloved Lover, our master the Chosen Prophet, the Light of insights and hearts, upon him be blessings and peace.

I ask God to grace this book of mine with acceptance, and make it a benefit for the Muslims in general and the faithful in particular. May He make it for us a covenant and bond with Him, for we had no other aim in writing it but securing His good pleasure. Nor did our pen move for any cause but obedience to His command and reverence of His rightful due, in return for the secrets of knowledge and mysteries of meaning that He entrusted to our heart.

This, then, is the printed book of Kāf. If your spirit yearns for dotted mystery, and if your innermost secret craves that which is concealed, then come and humble yourself at our doorstep. For it may be that you will attain the honor of entering the Presence, until we lead you at last to behold the Beloved, that you may return swiftly to the disclosure-site of the Day of Increase. God says, **faces that Day shall be radiant, gazing upon their Lord.**[1]

1st Rabīʿ al-Awwal 1440

10th November 2018

**Let this be our final call: "Praise be to God,
Lord of the worlds!"**[2]

1 Q Qiyāma 75:22-23.

2 Q Yūnus 10:10.

Bibliography

1. Albānī, Muḥammad Nāṣir al-Dīn, al-. *Ṣaḥīḥ al-jāmiʿ al-ṣaghīr wa-ziyādatuh*. Ed. Zuhayr al-Shāwish. Beirut: al-Maktab al-Islāmī, 1987.
2. ʿAjlūnī, Ismāʿīl b. Muḥammad, al-. *Kashf al-khafāʾ wa-muzīl al-ilbās ʿammā ishtahara min al-aḥādīth ʿalā alsinat al-nās*. Cairo: Maktabat al-Qudsī, 2010.
3. Asad, Muḥammad. *The Message of the Qurʾān*. Watsonville, CA: The Book Foundation, 2005.
4. Bayhaqī, Aḥmad b. al-Ḥusayn, al-. *Shuʿab al-īmān*. Ed. Ḥamdī al-Damardāsh, Muḥammad al-ʿAdl. Beirut: Dār al-Fikr, 2003.
5. Bukhārī, Muḥammad b. Ismāʿīl, al-. *Ṣaḥīḥ al-Bukhārī*. Beirut: Dār Iḥyāʾ al-Turāth al-ʿArabī, 2005 [?].
6. Corbin, Henry. *Creative Imagination in the Sufism of Ibn ʿArabī*. Trans. Ralph Manheim. Princeton: Princeton University Press, 1969.
7. Dāraquṭnī, ʿAlī b. ʿUmar, al-. *Sunan al-Dāraquṭnī*. Eds. ʿAlī Muhammad Muʿawwiḍ and ʿĀdil Aḥmad ʿAbd al-Mawjūd. Beirut: Dār al-maʿrifa, 2001.
8. Ḥākim, al-Nīshāpūrī, al-. *al-Mustadrak ʿalā al-Ṣaḥīḥayn*. Riyadh: Markaz al-turāth li-l-barmajiyyāt, 2013.

9. Ibn Abī ʿĀṣim, al-Ḍaḥḥāk. *Kitāb al-sunna*. Ed. Yaḥyā Murād. Beirut: Dār al-kutub al-ʿilmiyya, 2004.
10. Ibn ʿAdī, Abū Aḥmad al-Jurjānī. *al-Kāmil fī ḍuʿafāʾ al-rijāl*. Eds. ʿAlī Muḥammad Muʿawwiḍ and ʿĀdil Aḥmad ʿAbd al-Mawjūd. Beirut: Dār al-kutub al-ʿilmiyya, 1997.
11. Ibn ʿAjība, Aḥmad. *Al-Baḥr al-madīd fī tafsīr al-Qurʾān al-Majīd*. Beirut: Dār al-kutub al-ʿilmīya, 2002.
12. Ibn ʿArabī, Muḥyī al-Dīn. *al-Futūḥāt al-makkiyya*. Ed. ʿUthmān Yaḥyā. Cairo: al-Hayʾa al-miṣriyya al-ʿāmma li'l-kitāb, 1972.
13. Ibn Ḥanbal, Aḥmad. *Musnad al-Imām Aḥmad b. Ḥanbal*. Ed. Shuʿayb al-Arnāʾūṭ and ʿĀdil Murshid. Beirut: Dār al-risāla, 1995.
14. Ibn Ḥibbān, Muḥammad. *Ṣaḥīḥ Ibn Ḥibbān*. Ed. Shuʿayb al-Arnāʾūṭ. Beirut: Muʾassasat al-risāla, 1993.
15. Ibn Kathīr, Abū al-Fidāʾ Ismāʿīl b. ʿUmar. *Tafsīr al-Qurʾān al-*ʿaẓīm. Beirut: Dār Ibn Ḥazm, 1996.
16. Iskandarī, Ibn ʿAṭāʾ Allāh, al-. *al-Ḥikam al-ʿaṭāʾiyya al-kubrā wa'l-ṣughrā wa'l-munājāt al-ilāhiyya wa'l-mukātabāt*. Beirut: Dār al-kutub al-ʿilmiyya, 2017.
17. ———. *Ibn ʿAta'illah: The Book of Wisdom/ Kwaja Abdullah Ansari: Intimate Conversations*. Introduction, Translation, and Notes of the Book of Wisdom by Victor Danner and of Intimate Conversations by Wheeler M. Thackston. New York: Paulist Press, 1978.
18. Murata, Sachiko; Chittick, William. *The Vision of Islam*. London, New York: I.B. Tauris, 1994.

19. Muslim, Abū al-Ḥusayn b. al-Ḥajjāj al-Naysabūrī. *Ṣaḥīḥ Muslim*. Beirut: Dār iḥyā' al-kutub al-ʿarabiyya, 2012.
20. Nasā'ī, Aḥmad b. Shuʿayb, al. *Sunan*. Ed. ʿAbd al-Fattāh Abū Ghudda. Aleppo: Maktabat al-maṭbūʿāt al-islāmiyya, n/d.
21. Nasr, Seyyed Hossein; Dagli, Caner; Dakake, Maria Massi; Lumbard, Joseph; Rustom, Mohammed. *The Study Quran: a new translation and commentary*. New York, NY: HarperOne, an imprint of HarperCollins Publishers, 2017.
22. Nawawī, Yaḥyā b. Sharaf al-Dīn, al-. *Riyāḍ al-ṣāliḥīn*. Ed. Muḥammad Nāṣir al-Dīn al-Albānī. Beirut: al-Maktab al-islāmī, 1983.
23. Suyūṭī, Jalāl al-Dīn, al-. *al-Durar al-muntathira fī al-aḥādīth al-mushtahira*. Riyadh, Saudi Arabia: Jāmiʿat al-Malik Saʿūd, 2010.
24. ———. *al-Ḥāwī li'l-fatāwī*. Beirut: Dār al-kutub al-ʿilmiyya, 1975.
25. ———. *al-La'ālī al-maṣnūʿa fī al-aḥādīth al-mawḍūʿa*. Beirut: Dār al-maʿrifa, 1975.
26. Ṭabarānī, Sulaymān b. Aḥmad, al-. *al-Muʿjam al-kabīr*. Beirut: Dār al-kutub al-ʿilmiyya.
27. Tabrīzī, ʿAbd Allāh al-Khaṭīb, al-. *Mishkāt al-maṣābīḥ*. Beirut: al-Maktaba al-islāmiyya, 1985.
28. Tirmidhī, Muḥammad b. ʿĪsā, al-. *al-Jāmiʿ al-ṣaḥīḥ*. Ed. Aḥmad b. Muḥammad Shākir. Beirut: Dār al-kutub al-ʿilmiyya, 1987.

Index of Names

Index of Terms

A

B

C

D

E

T

U

V

W

Y

Z

BY THE SAME PUBLISHER

At the Service of Destiny

A Biography of the Living Moroccan Sufi Master Shaykh Mohamed Faouzi al-Karkari

....

In the Footsteps of Moses

A Contemporary Sufi Commentary on the Story of God's Confidant (kalīm Allāh) in the Qur'ān

....

Sufism Revived

A Contemporary Treatise on Divine Light, Prophecy and Sainthood

....

The Foundations of the Karkariya Order

Printed and bound
in the United States of America

www.ingramcontent.com/pod-product-compliance
Ingram Content Group UK Ltd.
Pitfield, Milton Keynes, MK11 3LW, UK
UKHW040603210726
13854UKWH00008B/1884

9 782930 978581